BRINGING JON HOME, THE

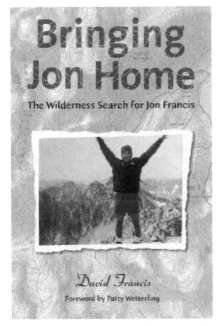

"I was devastated when I heard that Jon Francis was missing. I knew a lot about missing children, the response needed, how to work with law enforcement, how to engage the media. I had learned these things after my son Jacob was kidnapped and our family worked with so many —way too many—other searching families. But Jon's disappearance was different. As much as I wanted to help, I knew little about finding a missing adult on a mountain. David brilliantly captures the many stages of the search, of his family's grief, and of their process of remembering. If there was a person or resource to help anywhere, this amazing family found it and now offers that knowledge to others."

—Patty Wetterling, children's safety advocate, from the Foreword of *Bringing Jon Home*

"David Francis and his family engaged Minnesotans across the state from the governor to pilots they didn't even know in their search for Jon. Their personal bravery and persistence inspired all of us to help."

—Ann Rest, *Minnesota State Senate*

"*Bringing Jon Home* tells the story of a great young man, a son, a brother, and a friend who was taken from us at the very moment he was poised to do so much good; a true tragedy in the classic sense of the word. This story is a testament to the altruism that lives in all of those *unofficial* who moved heaven and earth."

—Cary Griffith, author of *Lost in the Wild*

"A father turns the tragedy of losing a loving son on a faraway mountaintop into a story of family, friends, strangers, communities all coming together to search and, ultimately, to embrace each other. This book becomes a reminder that none of us knows what tomorrow brings. But it also reminds us to appreciate the basic goodness around us—and to never forget to hug our kids. Every father should read this book."

—Doug Grow, Minneapolis *Star Tribune*

"*Bringing Jon Home* is a powerful story about loss, unconditional love and human resilience inside one American family."

—Chuck Logan, author of *Absolute Zero*

"A riveting read." —Mary Ann Grossmann, St. Paul *Pioneer Press*

". . . beautifully structured and written, each word glowing with sorrow and faith and love, a father's true testament of his son."

—Alla Renée Bozarth, PhD, author of *Life is Goodbye Life is Hello: Grieving Well through All Kinds of Loss.*"

"You've done a remarkable thing for Jon's legacy by not only capturing his giving, involved life, but offering his story as inspiration for other families. As a dad myself, I marvel at your resilience and strength. Your words are driven by the power of your emotion. I can feel it on every page."

—Kevin Giles, Minneapolis *Star Tribune*

GRIEF TRAVELERS

Learning to Live and Love Again after Loss

Peace and blessings on your journey.

David Francis

David Francis

Jon Francis Foundation
Stillwater, Minnesota
www.jonfrancisfoundation.org

Jon Francis Foundation
Post Office Box 2235
Stillwater, Minnesota 55082
www.jonfrancisfoundation.org

The book cover photo by Jon Francis was taken as he stood on the summit of the Grand Mogul on July 15, 2006. The photo was retrieved from his camera a year later.

This book is dedicated to Camille Francis, my
youngest grandchild.
She fills my heart with joy, love, and gratitude.
And
in memory of
Jonathan David Francis
He lived joyfully. He loved boldly.
(1982–2006)

CONTENTS

FOREWORD

Grief Travelers by David Francis has the authenticity of one who has
been on a long and arduous grief journey himself, following the death
of his only son in a mountain-climbing accident. The Jon Francis
Foundation grew out of David Francis' first, raw, heart-wrenching
account of the intense emotional work concurrent with the physical and
mental work in the years that immediately followed.

Finding a way to live meaningfully beyond grief is the most important and powerful aspect of grieving well. Activating the work of trans-
formation from devastation into the redemption of one's own life as a
survivor is the most courageous and vital work there is. In service to
other families, David Francis has been a saving grace in the example of
truthfulness he has set, as well as the help he has offered, passing on
help to others in the spirit which his son Jon showed by the way he
lived his brief but rich life.

In *Grief Travelers*, the author has given other travelers a cohesive
and logical arrangement of helpful counsel along the way. I believe his
most valuable offering is the recognition that there are no neat and tidy
methods of grieving. There is no rule book to follow. There is the way
that manifests for each person from within. But there are common
threads that weave across the loose patterns of mourning.

David Francis picks up those threads one by one and offers them to the reader. Some of those threads are strong and may be braided together by the reader to become lifelines.

—Alla Renée Bozarth, PhD, author of *Life is Goodbye/Life is Hello: Grieving Well through All Kinds of Loss,* and of *A Journey through Grief*

If I Could Mend Your Heart . . .

I would weave together
        the ragged edges
        of your threadbare heart
        and soothe your pain
        your shock
        and disbelief.

I would invite you to
        touch your sorrow
        and feel your feelings
        and not pretend to be strong
        or capable
        or composed.

I would listen without comment,
        to all that is unsettled
        in your soul
        your doubts
        your anger
        your fears
        about the future.

I would heed your cries
        and probing questions.
        What might you have done wrong or,
        what you might not
        have done at all.

For more than a single ending
    your loss may spark
    other sorrows
    other conclusions
    good-byes
    and
    thorny adjustments
    in every corner of your soul.

If I could mend your heart . . .
    I would promise not to say,
    "Look how well you're handling things,"
    or,
    "Cheer up.
    God wouldn't give you
    more than you could handle,"
    or,
    "You'll be over this soon."

Instead, I would whisper in your ear,
    "We live in a fragile and imperfect world
    tinged by brokenness
    and cloaked in
    unanswered questions.
    Some things truly aren't fair.
    This is hard."

For I don't think loss is about
    "handling things well,"
    or,
    "keeping it all together."

But about keeping afloat
in a rising tide of doubt.
Asking the silence,
"Why?"

"What is the meaning of this?"
It's about learning to co-exist with
an unwanted visitor,
with alien thoughts,
and depleted spirits.

If I could mend your heart . . .
I would draw you a plan and perfect map
to light your path from
confusion and despair
to
a place of new tomorrows
and rewarding journeys.

A place where anger could
release
its grip on understanding,
and anxiousness
might speak to acceptance.

I would shape for you
a fresh way
of seeing,
through prisms
of sunlight. . .

Prisms of sunlight that temper
            your pain with compassion
            and replace your doubts with faith,
            your grief with gratitude,
            your fear with trust.

If I could mend your heart . .
            I would open wide the doors of renewed hope
            —a hope much larger than wishes.
            One that waits,
            patiently,
            willingly,
            expectantly . . .

This fresh hope I send would
            let you step up with courage
            to the new day
            trusting that even pain can be
            transformed.

If I could mend your heart. . .
            I would lead you by the hand
            to this place of healing
            so that you might once again
            walk in your own path
            and make memories.

I would share with you a secret
            Joy is not about
            music
            and
            dance

and

laughter,

but about

the acceptance of Life.

Healing happens only where

fear and love,

joy and sorrow,

tears and smiles

can forge a

lasting peace.

The healing I speak of lies not in some safe place along the way,

but in

having made

the journey

stage

by

stage.

Until you reach that place,

a place

you may not now believe

exists,

I will save your space,

and watch with confidence

for your smiles yet to be.

—from *If I Could Mend Your Heart,* a healing book in the form of a poem
by The Reverend Mary I. Farr

INTRODUCTION

My son Jon's death in the wilderness drove me into deep darkness and despair. I was brought to my knees—weak and vulnerable. My brain was broken by depression and trauma. I felt severe pain and suffering because my only son was dead and his body was abandoned on a mountain.

I am a grief traveler. I was once crippled by intense feelings of anger, guilt, sorrow, betrayal, loneliness, and overwhelming grief. To continue to live and to love, I became a reluctant but dedicated student of loss in order to understand it and to attempt, desperately, to have some power over it. Consequently, I set out on a long and sorrowful journey.

Grief Travelers tells the story of my personal journey of sorrow, from mourning to healing. I include a few stories from my memoir, *Bringing Jon Home*, with personal insights and information on grief recovery from a variety of professionals and others who have experienced similar losses. I share lessons I have learned over the years since losing Jon— lessons from my personal heartbreaking experience as well as the study of the work and writings by grief experts, academics, and others I've met along the way who are also coping with the sorrow of loss. I include some of their stories as well.

If we did not love, we would not grieve. But love we do. Grief is the bleeding heart of love. Closure is a myth. Closure is for bank accounts, not love accounts. However, through our grief work, we can arrive at some resolution to the trauma caused by our loss. Untreated and/or unresolved grief can damage our faith and our mental and physical health. Grief is hard on our body, mind, and soul. Living in a fog of sorrow is debilitating. My religion and many other faiths teach us to reach out and do all we can to help others to heal from hurt. *Grief Travelers* is my offering in that regard.

The form of sorrow that I am most familiar with, and write about, is the death of a loved one. However, regardless of the cause of the loss, the healing process shares many similarities. On my journey, I learned that my approach is not the only way. In fact grieving is such a personal and often unpredictable experience that there may be more differences than similarities. However, I am sharing the roadmap I am following while I travel through the Valley of Grief.

I wrote *Bringing Jon Home* to put my pain on paper and to let others know that my only son, Jon Francis, once lived joyfully and loved boldly. My hope and purpose for writing *Grief Travelers* are first, that it may comfort, help, inspire, and empower my fellow grief travelers; and second, that it will support healthcare practitioners, clergy, and counselors in their important mission to listen and to heal others.

PART I

LOST

CHAPTER 1

MOUNTAIN OF LOSS

"So he told them this parable; What man of you, having a hundred sheep, if he has lost one of them, does not leave the ninety-nine in the wilderness, and go after the one that is lost, until he finds it?"   —Luke 15: 3–4 (RSV)

Jonathan David Francis was the son I had waited for most of my life. Linda and I had his name picked out for twenty-two years. Even as high school sweethearts, we talked about raising a family and decided to name our first son Jonathan David: Jonathan is Hebrew for "gift of God," and David means "beloved."

In the early morning of March 5, 1982, Jonathan David Francis was born. The doctor placed our son into his mother's arms. He had dark-brown hair, a handsome face, and sincere brown eyes that I thought reflected his Irish heritage. He joined our three daughters, Melissa, Jocelyn, and Robin. I believe God danced the day Jonathan was born.

Jon would have turned twenty-five on March 5, 2007. But we could not gather with him to celebrate his birthday that year. Jon was dead. He died alone on a mountain.

The Phone Call

Our home phone rang on Sunday, July 16, 2006, at 3:15 p.m. I was immediately happy seeing "Luther Heights" on the Caller ID; I assumed that our son Jon was calling home from the Idaho Bible Camp where he was working that summer as a counselor. But the person on the phone was not Jon.

The caller was the camp director whose voice was low and soft as he told me Jon had not returned to camp the previous night and wasn't at the morning staff meeting: "He's gone missing in the Sawtooth Mountains. The Custer County sheriff has called out a search party."

My knees went weak. As I repeated the horrifying news to Linda, we collapsed into a dark world of fear and desperation. Still clinging to each other, we agreed to go to Idaho to find Jon. Just before leaving, a deputy at the Custer County sheriff's office called to say they found Jon's car, but Jon was still missing. I called our daughters and told them we were leaving for Idaho. Each planned to join us as soon as possible.

Linda and I flew from Minneapolis/St. Paul to Denver, then Boise, and rented a car. Sometime in the night we stopped for rest at a motel in Twin Falls. Our eyes were too swollen from crying to sleep.

We drove a narrow, lonely, winding road the next morning to Stanley in Central Idaho and met with two Custer County sheriff deputies then drove to the "command center" at Sandy Beach on Redfish Lake. The search and rescue party had assembled that morning for the first full day of the search. The command post was a large white trailer surrounded by police vehicles, trucks, and uniformed sheriffs and forest service folks and others conversing in small groups.

Four men studied a map laid on the hood of a truck, and we heard voices over a radio. The county sheriff gave us a perfunctory greeting and turned away. The absence of any reassuring words added to our sense of desperation. Linda and I were weary and confused. We took refuge from the heat in the shade provided by a cluster of pine trees.

In a Fog of Sorrow

"This can't be happening," I said. "Jon was an experienced and fit climber—capable, and strong." I looked up at the mountain to the north, across the lake, the Grand Mogul, the mountain we were told that Jon left camp to climb two days earlier. I prayed to God and to the mountain for Jon's safe return. I ended each prayer with, *Jon, I love you.*

By midafternoon, when I could hold a thought for more than a few seconds, I began to focus more clearly on the search activity. I overheard the incident commander (IC) ask for status reports, repeating again and again on his radio, "Stay on safe and prescribed routes."

I walked over to the group standing over a map on the hood of a truck and introduced myself. One of the men, Erik, was from an organization called the Sawtooth Mountain Guides. The map was "The Sawtooth National Recreation Area." The men described the Grand Mogul terrain and the search locations. I understood very little of the conversation, but I thanked them and went back to my refuge in the shade with Linda.

Someone had retrieved Jon's copy of *Idaho: A Climbing Guide* by

Tom Lopez from Jon's cabin at Luther Heights Bible Camp. Jon had placed a bookmark on page 176, *The Grand Mogul*. After reading the Lopez pages, I approached the incident commander and asked for a briefing.

The IC described the routes of the dog teams and the ground search teams. He said that if Jon had followed the recommended Lopez route, he would have ascended the avalanche field to the northeast ridge. The Lopez book did not include a recommended descent route off the Grand Mogul.

"Has anyone been to the summit yet?" I asked. "Do we know if Jon made it to the summit?"

When the IC responded "no" to both questions, I entreated him to send someone to the summit. He turned to the large group of people standing around and asked for volunteers. Two eager searchers immediately came forward.

The newly formed search team set off, rode the sheriff's boat across Redfish Lake to the trailhead, climbed the Lopez route, and gained the summit of the Grand Mogul in less than three hours. On the summit, they discovered a registry in a rusty ammunition box where climbers who reach the peak can sign in. The search team reported back that they found a summit registry card inside the box filled out by Jon.

The team returned to Sandy Beach just before sunset and gave Jon's summit registry card to Linda. I stood in silence with my arm around Linda. In tears, she clung tightly to the handwritten note and read it over and over again.

07/15/06—Jon Francis, LHBC* and Ogden, Utah
Climbed avalanche field to east face and east ridge.
Great times bouldering!
All Glory to God for the climb and the beautiful Sawtooths.
*Luther Heights Bible Camp

After the evening search-team briefing, the IC came to me and said, "David, you need to be thinking about giving your son up to the mountain."

Incredulous, I felt a surge of anger. "No! You will not stop the search for Jon after only one day. You need to find him!"

The IC went back to the sheriff, then returned and said, "We'll search again tomorrow."

For the next hour, Linda and I drifted around lamely, thanking the searchers and petting the search dogs. As we drove slowly away from that mountain and the vacated search camp, Linda and I felt crushed by sadness and desperation. We headed to Stanley, where someone had booked us a room. For a second night, Linda and I held each other and cried.

Abandoned and Betrayed

Like the day before, Tuesday morning was hot in Central Idaho with a predicted high in the mid-nineties. Linda and I ate breakfast at the Mountain Village Restaurant mostly in silence, each in our own dark place. Our server, the mayor of Stanley, introduced herself and expressed her sympathy. I thanked her.

She smiled when I commented to her that I guessed she wasn't able to live on her mayor's pay. We left and drove to Sandy Beach for the second day of the search.

That morning, our daughter Jocelyn, son-in-law Doug Plass, and our grandchildren, three-year-old Audrey and one-year-old Charlie, arrived by car from California. They appeared tired too. I was so relieved to see them. I fell into a long hug and cry with Jocelyn.

Jocelyn and Doug sprang into action, meeting people and asking questions. Doug, tall and bearded, seemed to fit right in with the Idaho group. Jocelyn moved easily among the assembly, asking questions. Linda and I stayed in the shade with the kids, and I took a few trips to my crying rock facing the mountain.

Melissa's husband Steve, our newest son-in-law and a tall, fit, alpine skier, arrived from Minnesota. When a member of the official search team recommended that I charter a plane and fly over the mountain, Steve found a plane and a pilot from Challis Aviation to take us up.

While we prepared to fly over the Grand Mogul, the Custer County sheriff showed up and handed me an official candidate registration form for the Minnesota State Senate. By then, I'd been campaigning for the Minnesota State Senate for fifteen months and had earned the endorsement of the Minnesota Democratic Farmer Labor (DFL) party that spring.

My campaign manager had become aware that I had failed to register my intent to run, and she jumped through hoops to get the form to me in Idaho with detailed instructions on how to file.

I nearly tore up the form and threw it away. How could I finish a political campaign under these circumstances? But both of my sons-in-law, Doug and Steve, advised me to register. Doug cautioned, "Don't make an important decision like this in your state of mind." I put the registration form in my car.

Steve, Doug, and I climbed into the Cessna with Dave, our pilot. We taxied down the grass runway and took off. In less than ten minutes, we were over the Grand Mogul. The mountain loomed huge and ominous. We circled the granite mass repeatedly, trying to focus on rock surfaces. Bouncing in the updrafts made Doug and me airsick. I watched in amazement as Dave flew the plane, searched the mountain, and handed us airsickness bags.

After an hour in the air, we returned to the Stanley landing strip and lay down on the ground to recover. Reluctantly, I filled out the campaign registration form and faxed a notarized copy from the Challis Aviation office to the Minnesota Secretary of State.

Early in the afternoon, when we returned to Sandy Beach, search leaders were wrapping up the day's activities. I regretted taking that flight. It made us sick, wasted time and money, and took me away from the ground search. I felt angry and stupid.

Although I knew little about mountain search and rescue, I knew from my submarine "hide and seek" training in the US Navy that a search always restarts at the target's last-known position (LKP). Jon's LKP was the summit. That day's search should have focused on determining which descent route Jon took. Searchers should have gone up to the summit and back down all logical descent routes. But they were clearly not directed to do that.

My worst fears turned out to be true. The search leaders had concluded, without any physical evidence, that Jon was dead. When they failed to find him after a one-day search, they were now merely going through the motions. Since they were not being allowed to go off trail and to only use the "safe and prescribed routes," they couldn't search all logical descent routes. The more important objective of the officials was to end the search without injuries to any volunteers.

We were unaware at that time that county sheriffs are "kings" in their counties—not bound by any state or national standards. They can decide to search or to not search, and for how long. Custer County was not in the business of recovering the bodies of lost climbers. I hadn't seen this coming.

I remained silent when the IC looked at me directly and said for a second time, "David, it's time to give your son up to the mountain." I was immobilized by disbelief that they had come to this conclusion so quickly. I was paralyzed by a feeling of helplessness.

I concealed my anger that evening at the authorities for abandoning the search. At the final meeting of the official search team, I told the volunteers how much my family and I appreciated their dedicated work. Linda and I thanked each tired, distraught searcher. We shared a deep disappointment that we hadn't found Jon and brought him down from the mountain. They looked sad but resolved, and each one assured us they would return to find our son.

Linda and I sat on the dock with Erik's partner Kirk from the Sawtooth Mountain Guides. Kirk had been one of the spotters in a search helicopter. He kindly gave us Buddhist prayer flags and expressed his sympathy.

As the searchers hugged us and said their goodbyes, I fell deeper into the abyss of despair. I had learned during the search that a lost person who is not seriously injured and has a source of water could survive for up to seven days. Only three days had passed since Jon went missing. Jon could still be alive on that mountain! He could be waiting for us, expecting us to find and save him. We had begun to receive phone calls from psychics telling us Jon was still alive.

I yearned to go up on the mountain, cradle our son's body in my arms, and carry him away from this cruel and primitive place. But I knew nothing about search and rescue, and I had never in my life climbed a mountain. Only the sheriff had access to professional search-and-rescue resources. In my view, he squandered his authority and failed in his duty.

"The search for Francis ended at 7:50 p.m. St. Paul time," said the chief dispatcher for the Custer County sheriff's office. "The official search will not be resuming," said the dispatcher, who declined to give her name.
—Megan Boldt, St. Paul *Pioneer Press*. July 19, 2006.

Help

The Francis family gathered that night and decided to continue the search for Jon even though no local, state, or federal agencies would help us. We knew little about mountain climbing or search and rescue, but we would learn.

Hundreds of volunteers were streaming into Idaho to join the search for Jon. We created search teams and missions with dozens of Jon's friends, family friends, and people we'd never even met: Jon's running coaches and teammates; his friends from Lutheran churches, youth groups, and summer camps; strangers from Idaho and neighboring states; my friends, our daughter's friends, people from all across the US, and guests at the Redfish Lake Lodge; and some of the volunteers from the official search party who were eager to go back on the mountain. At our request, we were given the water-stained map that showed the "safe and prescribed routes" of the unsuccessful, twenty-nine-hour official search effort.

Now five days after Jon gained the summit of the Grand Mogul in the Sawtooth National Recreation Area, Idaho, we set up our makeshift command and control headquarters in the outdoor picnic area of the Redfish Lake Lodge. Owners of the lodge, Jeff and Audra, were gracious and supportive. Their rustic lodge offered shelter, bathroom facilities, food, and beverages. We plugged our electronics into the electrical outlet for the bandstand.

Jocelyn's husband Doug was appointed search manager because he had the most mountain-climbing experience, having climbed in the Rockies and the Sierras. Our oldest daughter, Robin, arrived from New York and took over media relations, her specialty. We were contacted hourly for interviews by newspapers, radio, and television reporters throughout the country. Boise Channel 7 parked a satellite TV transmission truck at the swimming beach on Redfish Lake.

Since neither the sheriff's office nor the Forest Service were required or willing to, Jocelyn created a handmade missing-person flier with Jon's picture. She alternated between angry wails and tears as she nailed pictures of her missing brother at trailheads in the Sawtooths, Stanley outfitters, and on Forest Service bulletin boards.

Linda took charge of the budget and spending necessary to pay for the search. She was banker, bookkeeper, treasurer, and travel agent. I handled most phone communications and logistics. Since our cellphones didn't work, we began calling Stanley, "communications hell." I struggled to stay on the line with then Governor Tim Pawlenty of Minnesota, who called to relay his concern for Jon and describe his efforts to restart the official Idaho search.

Jo Jo Fuller, on staff at the Redfish Lake Lodge, loaned us her satellite phone, which worked most of the time and reconnected us to the outside world. Another Redfish Lake Lodge staff member introduced herself; Greta had been on the morning shuttle boat ride with Jon on the five-mile trip across Redfish Lake to the Transfer Camp Site. Greta and her father, Tom, had taken family photographs on the boat, and Jon could be seen in the background wearing his favorite long-sleeved, aqua Coolmax shirt. I noticed the contemplative look on his face. I'd seen that look many times when he prepared for athletic competitions. Jon ran competitively for ten years and earned All State, All American, and National Championship honors. Before a race, he went deep and mentally prepared himself for the run. But this time, he was mentally preparing for a difficult solo mountain climb. Tom was the last person to speak with Jon before he began his climb that day. Tom recalled seeing Jon leave the shuttle boat and hike briskly to the trailhead leading to the Grand Mogul.

At family search headquarters, Pastor Dan Rieke, from Our Savior Lutheran Church in Twin Falls, Idaho, became our secretary. In a spiral notebook, he recorded information on volunteers and search assignments. He had met Jon at a weeklong, Bible Day Camp.

A friend of mine from Minnesota donated his corporate jet to fly in several searchers, two trackers, more of our family: our daughter Melissa and our grandchildren, ten-year-old Katie, and four-year-old Stephen. My friend, fellow Navy Reserve captain and mentor, Dave Recker, was also on that flight. His energy and enthusiasm immediately raised my spirits.

We were deluged with media interest and calls asking for information and/or offering help. I spent sixteen hours a day returning phone calls and screening and thanking volunteers while trying to stay on top of search tactics and clues. Many times, I stood in silent admiration watching our daughter Robin work. Confident and businesslike, she maintained grace under pressure. Cool in a crisis, she prepared press releases and handled media interviews and chaos.

Robin issued the first Francis family press release to a list of media contacts she assembled. The press release reflected our anger and desperation.

24-YEAR-OLD HIKER LOST:

IDAHO AUTHORITIES ABANDON SEARCH EARLY

Jon Francis, 24, last seen Saturday, Grand Mogul trail, Idaho.
Authorities call off search after only 2 days. Son of MN State Senate
Democratic Candidate David Francis, and employee of Luther Heights
Bible Camp.

Contact: Robin Francis

Twenty-four-year-old Jon Francis, of Stillwater, MN, set out Saturday
morning on a day hike up the Grand Mogul trail in rugged Sawtooth
Mountains, Idaho. He reached the summit but did not return. Francis,
an avid outdoorsman and experienced hiker, told friends at the Luther
Heights Bible Camp where he worked that he would return by 6:00
p.m. When he failed to show up, staff alerted authorities.

Sunday, the Custer County Sheriff's office launched a search party
but abandoned efforts Tuesday night after only 2 days, leaving Francis's
family and friends to continue the search alone. Jon is the son of David
Francis, a Democratic candidate for Minnesota State Senate, who
immediately flew to Idaho with friends and family to lead an
independent search for Jon. Jon is described as deeply religious and
mature. Distraught friends and family are pouring into Idaho to
continue the daylight search, but more manpower and official support
are needed.

Tourism to Idaho State Parks is the state's third-leading industry
hosting over two million visitors a year, but are tourists and outdoor
enthusiasts really safe? Authorities provided a conservative search but

simply gave up when initial efforts failed to locate Francis. Idaho authorities only explored the summit, where Francis was last seen, after urging from David Francis.

The Francis family and friends believe Jon is alive and in need of immediate assistance; Minnesota residents are outraged and engaged. Minnesota congressmen and senators are talking with counterparts in Idaho; Episcopal and Lutheran bishops are working with Idaho delegations and contacting the governor as friends and family come to Idaho to launch a search for Francis.

The Francis family urges State officials to re-engage their search, and they call for the help of experienced hikers and guides to locate their missing son.

FIND JON: Keep Idaho Looking

We felt uplifted when our first volunteer dog handler and search dog arrived: Jim Hanley and his dog Shania, a border collie from South Dakota. Jim, wearing an Australian slouch hat, looked like he had arrived from the outback. He was immediately surrounded by a crowd of volunteers who welcomed him warmly. When I asked Jim about Shania's capabilities, we soon discovered we were "fraternity brothers." A former Navy corpsman; he immediately assumed the role of first-aid person and treated a cut I had on my leg, recognizing that I was under emotional distress at "my battle station" but working hard to organize the operation. Linda and I hoped that Jim's search dog would lead us to Jon's chosen descent route.

Unfortunately, Shania's early efforts yielded no clues.

Dozens of friends and volunteers arrived with provisions and equipment including much-needed two-way radios. Many sat quietly with us in prayer. Tom and Nancy Austin, from our church in Stillwater, arrived. She cooked while he climbed.

Within a few days, we managed to organize and send 120 "heartbeats" (a person or a dog) onto the Grand Mogul and bring them all back safely. Several heartbeats searched multiple times. We suffered only one minor injury that week. Doug's friend John from Washington State fell and cut his nose, requiring six stitches.

Meanwhile, the television reporter from Channel 7 in Boise told me the Republican acting governor of Idaho, Lieutenant Governor James Risch, was coming to Redfish Lake to meet with us. I was annoyed—we needed search dogs, not politicians. Although I was concerned about this distraction from our efforts, I felt a faint hope that the governor might bring more resources to help us find Jon.

The Ambush

At the end of Day 6, when all our searchers were safely off the mountain, Linda, Robin, and I sat on the Redfish Lake dock waiting for the governor of Idaho. We had not been given a time or a meeting place.

Jim Risch had been Lieutenant Governor of Idaho until May 2006 when he replaced Governor Dirk Kempthorne, who became President George W. Bush's Secretary of the Interior. The sun was setting when a sheriff's deputy arrived to inform us that Governor Risch was waiting for us at the Redfish Lake Visitor's Center. We had no idea where that was, so we followed the deputy in our car.

Once in the Visitor's Center conference room, we found ourselves in an ambush, surrounded by state officials and law enforcement officers in uniform. Mrs. Risch, fashionably dressed, was the one friendly face in the room. She greeted us warmly and expressed her condolences. Governor Risch sat at the head of the table. Dressed in coat and tie, Risch was a slim, balding man. He rose to shake my hand.

I immediately felt ill-prepared for the meeting. I had spent the entire day immersed in a desperate search for my son; I was hardly ready for a business meeting with the Idaho governor and his entourage. In my thirty years of military, public, and business experience, I planned and led many important meetings. I had told truth to power and faced tough negotiators. But that evening, I was a grieving father—groping in a fog of sorrow—and we were ambushed. We were quickly broadsided with the governor's scripted message that the Francis family was risking the lives of others by continuing our search without professional resources.

I responded by stating the obvious: that we were desperately *trying* to get professional Search and Rescue personnel—especially search dogs—but they would not come to our aid without the sheriff's authorization—and that the Custer County sheriff would not provide authorization. I added that our efforts were being hampered by State-sponsored radio announcements telling people not to come to Idaho to help search for Jon Francis. At one point, Robin saw the sheriff and the incident commander roll their eyes.

The governor repeated the scripted message—that the official search was over, and if we continued to put people on the mountain, the Francis family would be responsible for any injuries or deaths. At the end of his monologue, we were asked to step outside while the officials reached a decision concerning any further Idaho State action.

When we were ushered back into the conference room, the governor said Idaho would provide us with search aircraft and a National Guard communications truck over the weekend. I thanked the governor, and we left.

Immediately after the meeting, I regretted not giving voice to my family's pain. I wish I had been able to say, "Governor, if that were your son on the Grand Mogul, would you be satisfied with a two-day search resulting in no recovery?" And, "Governor, you wouldn't have had to travel all this way if the sheriff had done his job." Or, "Sheriff, you are an elected official responsible for search and rescue in a county that is 80 percent wilderness. Your lack of resources, preparation, effort, and commitment borders on negligence and dereliction of duty."

On Day 7, July 21, 2006, the last day, in my mind, our son could still be alive, we were ordered off the mountain to prevent interference between ground searchers and aircraft. We were given no information from state or local authorities. Everything we learned came from the media. The governor had deployed helicopters with infrared and search aircraft with spectral imaging technology. We wanted to place feet, eyes, and noses on the mountain that day, not questionable technology. We sat in frustration as a helicopter with heat-seeking capabilities flew over the sun-baked mountain during the hottest part of the day. As a Navy Reserve officer, I knew that we were simply providing a training weekend for an Idaho National Guard Unit.

The aircraft found nothing. We eventually learned that in a wilderness search for a non-responsive, missing person, helicopters and search aircraft are the least effective. All we could do was to document the pointless activities that prevented us from searching on the mountain:

Ryan Jung, one of the Sawtooth Mountain guides, had ridden in the helicopter, and he described his frustration regarding the five-and-a-half-hour search. In an interview afterward with Dana Dugan of the *Idaho Mountain Express,* he said, "The crew engineer operated the forward-looking infrared system, known as FLIR. The screen is only 7 to 8 inches. It's good for surveillance or to stop intruders, but it doesn't work for looking in three-dimensional topography. The human eye is more sensitive to color. I asked if a body would show, and the crew said it wouldn't."

Clearly, the governor was a skillful politician and an artful dodger. In the public eye, he had responded to political pressure, come to the rescue of local law enforcement, and appeared to be providing help in our time of need. But we needed people and dogs. What we got was an ambush and political air cover for Idaho's elected officials.

By Day 8, Jon was most likely no longer alive.

When the Idaho National Guard communications truck arrived, I stepped inside to use the high-tech communications devices to maintain contact with the search parties and return dozens of phone messages. But the sergeant said, "No. I'm sorry you can't stay in here. You are not authorized. We will put a telephone outside for you."

So I took a seat at a card table set outside with a telephone. The surroundings looked like a law enforcement convention. As the Francis family volunteers were allowed back on the mountain, dozens of official observers stood watch. The superintendent of the Minnesota Bureau of Criminal Apprehension had flown out two BCA agents to be with us. Several county sheriffs and deputies stood around with their hands on their gun belts. Though it appeared as if we had more observers than searchers, we put more volunteers on the mountain Saturday and Sunday who searched the summit, the east side, the west side, portions of the south, and parts of the north face. But the wide search failed to find any trace of Jon.

I was too numb to mourn the death of our only son. I needed to deal with the politics swirling around my head. I became concerned that our public expressions of anger at Idaho officials might be misinterpreted as a lack of appreciation for the outpouring of support from countless Idaho volunteers. Robin wrote a new press release that expressed our sincere gratitude to the Idaho volunteers.

Vigils

By late Sunday afternoon, July 23, eight days after Jon went missing, we were mentally and physically exhausted. I ached with the knowledge that Jon was gone. Never again could I hold him, hug him, or hear him call me Dad. I was robbed of his presence and his future.

That evening, after all of the searchers were safely off the mountain, Doug came to me in tears, saying, "David, we didn't find Jon. I'm sorry." As I embraced my son-in-law, I thanked him for his awesome effort and love.

We gathered in a circle on the Shore of Redfish Lake in view of the Grand Mogul. Pastor Dan led us in prayer. His words were comforting and wrenching. For the first time since Linda and I arrived in Idaho, the sky looked dark, angry, and ominous. As black clouds hovered over the Grand Mogul, I directed my thoughts again and again toward the mountain: *Jon, I love you. Jon, I miss you. I lift you up and place you in the arms of God.* Finally, I asked in lament, *God, where were you? Why didn't you guide Jon's feet off that mountain?*

Our family said thank you and farewell to the last of the volunteers. We drove as if in a funeral procession to Sawtooth City where Jocelyn had rented a house for the family. We were all together—our three daughters, two sons-in-laws, and four grandchildren. But we were not complete. Jon wasn't there.

Sawtooth City, population fifteen, situated near Smiley Creek, is about twenty miles south of Stanley. We now had access to a landline telephone; I sat at the kitchen table and returned dozens of calls. I returned several calls from the Episcopal Bishop of Minnesota. Bishop Jelinek knew Jon from his involvement with a Diocesan Youth Group.

They had traveled to Washington DC together on a pilgrimage to the National Cathedral. Bishop Jelinek had written letters and made phone calls to the governor, senators, and representatives of Idaho, encouraging the officials to renew the search for Jon.

I returned phone messages from members of the Minnesota State Legislature: Senate Majority Leader Dean Johnson (also a Lutheran pastor and a brigadier general, Chaplain Corps, Minnesota National Guard), and State Senators Ann Rest and Becky Lourey (a Gold Star Mother whose son was killed in Iraq).

There were messages from Minnesota Governor Tim Pawlenty; Minnesota's Commissioner of Public Safety, Michael Campion; members of the Minnesota Congressional Delegation who had lobbied their counterparts in Idaho to continue the search; messages of support and sympathy from Episcopal and Lutheran church leaders as well as members; friends, relatives, and countless friends of Jon. We received offers of sympathy and help from many people I didn't know.

Patty Wetterling called to express her sympathy and to extend an offer of help from the Jacob Wetterling Foundation (JWF). Patty and her husband Jerry were the first to send me a copy of The Reverend Mary Farr's incredible book, *If I Could Mend Your Heart.*

Patty and Jerry had established JWF in February of 1990, four months after their eleven-year-old son, Jacob, was abducted at gunpoint by a masked man near the Wetterling home in St. Joseph, Minnesota. JWF became the Jacob Wetterling Resource Center (JWRC) in 2008 to carry on the work of finding missing children and educating children, teens, parents, caregivers, and teachers about personal safety. (Jacob's disappearance remained an agonizing mystery for nearly twenty-seven years! In September 2016, a longtime suspect finally confessed to the kidnapping and murder of Jacob, and his body was recovered. The killer was sentenced to twenty years in prison.)

Father Jerry Doherty, our priest at Ascension Episcopal Church in Stillwater and one of my closest friends and confidants, and others had led a candlelight vigil at Ascension Church in Stillwater, shortly after Jon went missing. Jerry had known him since Jon was nine, and Jon had worked for him one summer. Our families had camped together in the Boundary Waters Canoe Area Wilderness in Northern Minnesota. Jerry flew to Idaho to be with us, and we met the next day at Luther Heights Bible Camp. I felt immediately comforted by his presence.

That day was another in what seemed to be an endless series of beautiful days—almost a perfect day. The sun was bright in a cloudless, crystal-blue sky. The air was warm; the winds light. We were surrounded by beauty—snow-capped mountains, lush pine trees, and a shimmering lake. But I resented all of the perfection. This was the lake that carried Jon to the mountain. The tall trees watched silently as he climbed. "All Glory to God for the beautiful Sawtooths," Jon had written on the mountaintop that I now regarded as soulless and savage.

Father Jerry was able to express the anger, confusion, and sense of outrage that afflicted all of us. He had lived and ministered in Montana for many years and understood the Western culture that seemed willing to bow to the mystique and power of the mountain—and believe that it was a beautiful place to die. I didn't share that sentiment. Jerry and I agreed that abandoning a loved one on a mountain was insane.

I had to hold my anger in check whenever someone said to me, "Jon is in a beautiful place. It is where he wanted to be." A few times, I found the courage to reply, "No. Jon wanted to come down from the mountain and go back to camp to do the work he enjoyed with the youth he loved."

I was never able to say aloud the truth that lived in the darkest corner of my mind: *This mountain is not a beautiful place. My son's body is now at the bottom of the food chain where it will be destroyed by the elements and devoured by predators!*

Father Jerry and my family took the shuttle boat on a pilgrimage to the foot of the Grand Mogul. In sight of the mountain's north face, Jerry read from Psalm 121. Together we cried, prayed, and stared mindlessly at the mountain. To me it felt like a funeral for Jon. I was parting with my son. I was saying goodbye. I was releasing him.

A Song of Ascents

I lift up my eyes to the hills—
from where will my help come?
My help comes from the LORD,
who made heaven and earth.
He will not let your foot be moved;
he who keeps you will not slumber.

He who keeps Israel

will neither slumber nor sleep.

The LORD is your keeper;

the LORD is your shade at your right hand.

The sun shall not strike you by day,

nor the moon by night.

The LORD will keep you from all evil;

he will keep your life.

The LORD will keep

your going out and your coming in

from this time on and forevermore.

—Psalm 121: 1–8

One by one, we talked about Jon, how much we loved him, and what a difference he made in our lives. Melissa added that she couldn't remember a time when her brother complained about another person— he met people wherever they were and loved them as they were. I saw that in Jon too.

Our grandchildren wanted to go swimming, so Melissa took them into the cold water of the lake. As I watched my young grandchildren playing in the water, I saw life. But when I looked up, I saw only death, the stark mountain of loss.

Luther Heights Bible Camp

Our next vigil was several days later at Luther Heights Bible Camp where Jon spent four wonderful summers as a counselor. We met his friends, mentors, and staff; all were in shock and mourning. We found Jon's friend and frequent climbing partner, Cara, alone and crying under a cluster of trees. Linda and I went with camp leaders and staff across Redfish Lake again to the Transfer Camp and sat in a circle around a campfire pit. I thought back to the many campfires over the years sitting with Jon and our extended family telling stories, staring into the fire, feeling close and content.

Here there was no campfire, but Jon's friends told stories about him. We listened to examples of how Jon brought love, joy, and fun to all his relationships. His mentor, Laura, shared that Jon told her he'd finally made a decision to attend seminary to become a pastor. I knew Jon had been struggling with a sense of call to ordained ministry. I felt pride at the news, and pain that he would not complete his goal.

During this campfire circle, I began to see Jon not as my little boy, but as a man, a remarkable young man who loved deeply and was deeply loved. *How did I miss knowing this?*

We left the fire circle vigil and returned to Sawtooth City. We needed to make tough decisions to continue the search. First we decided to engage Erik Leidecker and the Sawtooth Mountain Guides (SMG) to help and advise us on continuing search efforts. They knew the Sawtooths better than anyone.

Erik was intelligent, experienced, and fit. He was a Dartmouth graduate, a literature major who combined his passion—back country activities—with his occupation. Erik and his partner Kirk led white-water rafting trips, mountain climbing, backpacking, and wilderness hiking and camping groups. He enjoyed extreme sports like winter skiing on the Sawtooth slopes. Although he was compassionate, he was also realistic about SMG's limited ability to find Jon.

The Sawtooth Mountain Guides spent several days climbing and searching. They reported a foul smell detectable by the human nose and attempted to locate it. I tried to push out of my mind the horrible image this created. Jon's body was now decomposing. Our son's remains were attracting scavengers. We needed to find him before his body was stolen from us.

Journey of Sorrow

In early August, we were unable to put together a search effort. Leaving Idaho, Linda and I were unwilling pilgrims on a journey of sorrow. First, we returned to Luther Heights Bible Camp to gather Jon's belongings. We met again with staff and campers who were still in tears and shock. We attended chapel at the camp and ate dinner in the dining hall. I climbed to the highest point called the "Rock" where Jon had lingered many times. I sat looking over the awesome landscape and cried.

The cabins at Luther Heights Bible Camp are named after Idaho summits: Blackman, Braxon, Castle, Horton, Hortsmann, Hyndmann, Patterson, Snowyside, Thompson, Washington, Williams, etc. Jon had climbed most of the mountains with friends from camp. Some he climbed more than once. I found his handwritten list, as a bookmark, in his copy of the Lopez book. Jon had also gained the highest summit in Idaho, 12,655-foot Mount Borah in the White Cloud Mountains. Perhaps like Moses, Abraham, and Jesus, Jon went up the mountain to seek God's mind. I can't be sure, but I do know that Jon believed the mountains throbbed with the heart of God.

We visited all of the camp places Jon had been, regarding them all as sacred spaces. In the sparse cabin where he had slept, we found his set of keys—to the house, car, and church. Reverently, I buried my nose in my son's clothing to inhale his familiar fragrance. We packed his things into his car, a green Subaru Outback he had recently purchased—his first car. Except for what he carried with him up the Grand Mogul on July 15, 2006, Jon's car now held everything he had taken with him to Idaho. At nightfall, we left Luther Heights for our drive to Ogden, Utah, where Jon had been serving as director of youth ministry at Ascension Lutheran Church.

Ogden is surrounded by mountains, forests, hiking trails, and water. I could see why Jon loved living in Utah. I could imagine him canoeing, kayaking, skiing, and mountain climbing in this outdoor mecca. Linda and I had not met Jon's new congregation, his pastor, or the youth group until we arrived in Ogden.

Jon had rented a room from one of Ascension's members. Joanna, a computer programmer, was a middle-aged, gentle and soft-spoken single woman. She joined us for lunch and told us how much she appreciated Jon's presence in her home and enjoyed hiking, climbing, and skiing with him.

The people of Ascension Lutheran shared our despair and disbelief.

Linda and I were awash in the love and grief of Jon's congregation. We met with Jon's youth group in the room that they had painted in bright fluorescent colors and decorated with scripture. A shocking lime-green wall had "God Loves You" painted in large blue letters.

The young people wore white ribbons with "Jon Francis" printed on them. Kids gave us balloons and cards with written notes to Jon, expressing their love for him and their anguish that they would never be able to see him again. For many of these kids, this was the first time in their lives that they had encountered a loss this painful—the unresolved loss of a teacher, mentor, and friend. Behind tears and brave faces, they told stories about Jon. He was not much older than they were, but he lived an authentic, faith-filled life that they admired. He talked the talk and walked the walk. He brought fun and joy into their lives. The depth and strength of his ministry were evident. He told them about his faith and taught the gospel with deep conviction. He was real, and he was never boring.

The kids told stories about how competitive Jon could be on the playing field. I told them my own tale of how Jon tried to knock me out of our family football games, and how he roughhoused with his sisters. During our backyard football games, touch often turned into tackle. Jonathan preferred to play on the team opposing me so he could take occasional shots at me. During one game, he hit me so hard I flew horizontally through the air and landed five feet away. "Jon if you do that again, you'll be grounded," his mother had shouted at her twenty-one-year-old son.

A church leader told us how Jon had helped organize the annual Ascension 5K Grace Race that spring. Jon had finished first, set a new course record, then circled back on the course to encourage other runners.

Several members of Ascension were mountain climbers, and some were search-and-rescue professionals. A few reminded me that they had been with us in Idaho in July and wanted to continue the search for Jon. I thanked them all, and we set a date in late August to meet in Stanley.

Linda and I drove to Joanna's house. Packing up our son's personal belongings was a gut-wrenching experience. Our hands often shook as we touched, smelled, read, caressed, cried over, and eventually placed in boxes Jon's clothing, letters, books, CDs, pictures, sports equipment, and his applications to seminaries.

I found his registration and entry form for the November 2006 Seattle Marathon. I instantly knew why he picked Seattle for his second marathon. Alexis Nelson, his high school sweetheart, lived there. We performed the same sorrowful task at Jon's office at the church. I found the laptop computer I gave him for college. But I could not bring myself to open it or look at any of his files.

On August 16, Ascension Lutheran held a memorial service for Jon. We were told of similar prayer vigils for Jon being held in churches across the country.

Pastor David Kiel sent me his message to his congregation about Jon:

We are here today to give thanks to God for the life of Jonathan David Francis! Jon did not live for himself. He loved the Lord. We all knew that . . . we all saw that. His whole life was about loving and serving God by loving and serving God's people. That's why he worked at a Christian camp. That is why he served this congregation as our minister of youth. That is why he led groups of people to work at Habitat for Humanity and to serve those less fortunate at St. Anne's Center here in Ogden. That's why Jon was coming back to Ascension after being at camp this summer and having worked at camp at least four summers in a row. That is why Jon was planning on going to seminary in a year. He loved the Lord, and he lived for the Lord."

Jon loved life! We saw it. We experienced it. His love for life made us all smile! And we all know that his love for life was grounded deeply in his love for God. Jon lived an abundant life—and it was abundant because he was a servant of Christ. It gave his life purpose and meaning.

That's why Jon was so endearing to us. That's why we can thank God for him. That's why we can celebrate Jon this day in the midst of what we don't understand—in the midst of our sadness—in the midst of our loss.

Jon—we love you and we miss you deeply! Please know that you made a difference in our lives. Please know that you touched us all with the love of God. We will spend the rest of our lives in an attempt to honor you by serving each other just as you served us! We thank God for you, and we'll carry you in our hearts always!

We ran out of room inside Jon's Subaru, so we bought a car-top carrier, and Joanna rigged a makeshift bike carrier for Jon's mountain bike. We said goodbye, hugged Joanna, and thanked her for being a good friend to our son. Linda and I headed east toward Minnesota. When she drove, I sat in the passenger seat and cried. We switched, and it was her turn to cry.

Late one day, while driving across Nebraska, we decided to stop for the night. We were in Lincoln where Jon ran a marathon in 2005. As I pulled off the Interstate, Linda and I both gasped immediately when we recognized the same hotel where we stayed with Jon. We had no tolerance at that moment for any reminders of good times with Jon. I circled around and drove on to the next exit.

When we arrived in Minnesota, our neighbors greeted us and helped us unload Jon's car. We neatly and carefully placed Jon's belongings in the garage. We needed time to decide where his things would be stored. Linda went upstairs to put the Ascension balloons and love notes in Jon's bedroom.

The following day, Linda and I began responding to the hundreds of cards, letters, phone messages, and donations. We found many copies of the St. Paul, Minneapolis, and Stillwater newspapers that contained articles on Jon's disappearance. I didn't realize until then the intense level of outrage that was felt by so many in Minnesota toward the Idaho officials in response to their decision to abruptly stop the search for Jon.

CHAPTER 2

JON'S HEART

A reader of my memoir, *Bringing Jon Home,* sent me a note that said, "David, I didn't understand the depth of your loss until I read the chapters about your amazing son." Writing that book carried me through Jon's life and played a large part in the progression of my grief travels.

Our daughters, neighbors, and friends were so excited when we brought newborn Jonathan home from the hospital. Jonathan made me feel whole. We had three beautiful daughters, ages eleven, fourteen, and sixteen, and now the son Linda and I had held in our hearts for twenty-two years. From the beginning, Jon's sisters surrounded him with love and attention, cuddled him, watched over him, and dressed and fed him.

When our daughters were babies, I was in the US Navy, going to sea as a submarine sailor and later as an officer. While I was on active duty, Linda and I had three children in five years, but I was seldom home to help with our girls. I missed so much of the joy *and the hard work* of their early months. Jonathan was my chance to be present during the baby months. I cherished that time—the baths, nighttime feedings, even diaper changes. I rocked and caressed Jonathan and fed him his supplemental bottle, relishing our time together in the quiet beauty of the night.

Because Easter arrived shortly after Jonathan's birth, we prepared for his baptism, and the confirmation of fourteen-year-old Jocelyn at the Great Vigil of Easter in April 1982. Their combined spiritual rituals were a portent of the close relationship that grew between Jocelyn and Jon. The Francis family gathered at the 120-year-old stone Cathedral of Our Merciful Saviour in Faribault, Minnesota, which was filled to capacity with Easter worshippers. The Easter Vigil is the most ancient and beautiful of Christian celebrations—a service resplendent with music, scripture, tradition, and sacraments of baptism, confirmation, and Eucharist (Holy Communion).

Jonathan, dressed in white, was baptized with water and the Holy Spirit in the stone baptismal font by our priest and friend from Holy Cross Church in Dundas, the Reverend Jim Newman. John and Coralie, Jonathan's godparents, our daughters and my mother, Millie, stood with us as we reaffirmed our baptismal covenant and renounced evil. Near the stained-glass window of Jesus the Good Shepherd holding a lamb, Jonathan was anointed with oil and sealed by the Holy Spirit—marked as Christ's own forever.

Jocelyn was confirmed the same evening. The bishop placed his hands on her head, passing down the ancient Christian sacrament of initiation into the assembly of the faithful. We received communion, celebrating the memorial of our redemption, recalling Christ's death, and proclaiming his resurrection and ascension. The Easter Vigil lasted more than three hours. My mother, a Baptist, turned to me several times during the service to ask, "Is it over yet?"

Jonathan's life in the Spirit was planted that day. When, at age two, he and Linda walked past the cathedral where he had been baptized, he looked up at the impressive building and said, "Look! It's King Friday's castle!" (from *Mr. Rogers' Neighborhood*)

"No, Jonathan, that's the church where you were baptized," his mother replied.

"With water and the Holy Spirit!" he responded confidently.

The next year we had a daughter in college and a son in diapers. One of my favorite roles was "bath giver." We played with Biblical bathtub toys: Noah's Ark, and Jonah and the whale.

I enjoyed Dr. Seuss books as much as Jonathan did. Among our favorite bedtime stories were the Jibboo, from *Oh! The Thinks You Can Think!* and *The Lorax*. The Lorax spoke for the trees, and his voice spoke directly to Jonathan. He especially loved *Oh, the Places You'll Go!*

After all three of our daughters left home for college, we downsized. We moved from Northfield to our new country home built on three acres just north of Stillwater, Minnesota. We chose Stillwater because it's a great "village"—a small town of about eighteen-thousand people nestled in wooded hills in the scenic St. Croix River Valley.

Jonathan made a graceful transition and immediately fell in love with the rural environment and his open school, Stonebridge Elementary. He thrived in the self-paced atmosphere. At Stonebridge, we witnessed the personal discipline, work ethic, integrity, and self-regulated behavior that became hallmarks of his character.

He brought home information about environmental damage done by phosphates in lawn fertilizers. I learned from him about the use of corn gluten meal, an environmentally safe natural weed suppressant and fertilizer. It worked!

Gently and persistently, our young son taught us how to be more environmentally sensitive and take positive actions. We found and used organic and safe recipes for every purpose. We planted trees—more than fifty pine seedlings. Our soil was so inert that few survived, but our Macintosh apple tree flourished.

Jonathan was eight when we made our first trip to the pristine Boundary Waters Canoe Area Wilderness in Northern Minnesota. The area covers more than a million acres, extending nearly 150 miles along the Canadian border, with more than twelve hundred miles of canoe routes and 2,000 campsites. While still paddling in the middle of a large lake and looking for a campsite, Jonathan and I battled high winds and choppy waters. Jonathan, in front, struggled to keep us on course. I was proud of his tenacious grit.

I witnessed Jonathan's true love and respect for nature that summer when he caught a twelve-inch Northern Pike, a bony fish we decided not to eat. He built a stone pond in the lake for the fish and watched it swim around for a few hours before releasing it back into the deep water. We made several more trips together to the Boundary Waters, often on Father's Day weekend.

Jon teased before each departure, "Dad, have you over-packed yet for our camping trip?"

At the dinner table, one evening, thirteen-year-old Jonathan announced that he didn't want to be called Jonathan anymore. His name would be Jon. From then on, we called him Jon, most of the time.

Wired to Run

Jon's growth as an athlete revealed a great deal about how his character developed over the years. I was his soccer coach for six years. He handled that gracefully and was always respectful to his dad/coach. I watched Jon evolve into an accomplished athlete. He had seen me run competitively for many years and began to express interest.

When he finished second at the Stonebridge one-mile in sixth grade, I sensed he had a gift. Our first race together was the Marine on St. Croix two-mile run. Jon was eleven. We ran side by side and finished together.

In eighth grade, Jon was one of the fastest runners in his class. By ninth grade, he was drafted for high school varsity track. Scott Christensen, an outstanding hall of fame high school coach, nurtured Jon's natural talent and work ethic. Scott told us that Jon was wired to run.

As a fifteen-year-old high school sophomore, Jon earned a top spot on the high school varsity boy's cross-country team and helped lead it to a state and national championship. The 1997 Stillwater High School

Boys Cross Country Team went undefeated. They were Conference, Section, and State Champions, and voted by the sports writers (*USA Today/Harrier's*) as National Champions (Ranked first of 23,000 high school boys teams). Jon finished eighth at the sectional, completing the 5K course in 16:18, and qualifying for his first Minnesota State Meet.

"You smell like a wet dog," Jocelyn once said to Jon when he returned home after a run and the nickname stuck. The entire family started calling him Jon Dog.

The movie *Chariots of Fire* was Jon Dog's favorite movie—the true story of Eric Liddell and Harold Abrahams, two men driven by the need to run, exhibited exceptional speed and trained passionately to compete in the 1924 Olympics. Eric Liddell, a Protestant missionary from Scotland, said he ran "for the glory of God." After winning Olympic medals in France, Eric traded glory and applause for an opportunity to preach the gospel as a missionary.

Jon watched that movie the night before every big race. Running was also an expression of his faith. He had a gift and, like Eric Liddell, he ran to glorify God. Inside Jon's CD soundtrack of *Chariots of Fire*, he wrote: "Where does the power come from to see the race to its end? From within."

When Jon was a senior in high school, Linda and I arrived at the sectional meet on a cold October afternoon. At the start, Jon moved to the front. He was out to run a personal best time and earn a spot at the State meet. His lead was so large, he appeared to be running the race alone. Jon was "in the zone" and did not recognize that the golf cart driver took a wrong turn leading Jon and a handful of other runners on a two-hundred-yard detour.

Jon regained the course and ran a blistering pace to catch up and finish eleventh. Unfortunately, only the top ten finishers go to State. We, and all Stillwater fans, were outraged at what the incompetent cart driver did to Jon. But Jon said, "No. It was my fault. I should have known the course better."

This example of Jon's character, along with his competitive spirit, were no doubt what Jon's peers recognized when he was elected captain of both his high school and college track and cross country teams. The running road trips were often long, but always enjoyable. We traveled all over the US for track and cross country meets and races. In addition to his high school running, Jon competed in Foot Locker and Junior Olympics.

I had the pleasure of running several races with him. One spring morning, we rose early and ran a 10K together. Jon finished second. I finished around two-hundredth. Waiting at the finish line, Jon greeted me, "Hey, Dad, I didn't expect you back so soon!"

After Jon died, I reached out to his friends to feel closer to my son, and as a result I learned much more about him—what he was like as a friend, how others perceived him, and how his heart and his character were recognized by others.

Jon's close friend Kevin was Jon's teammate and running partner in high school. Both were talented runners who were grouped together in workouts. They had a tight-knit and respectful bond even though they were a year apart and had a different circle of friends. Jon was shorter in stature; Kevin towered over him by a foot. Kevin was teased that Jon must be a better athlete because he had to take twice as many strides for every one Kevin took.

Kevin described the nature of their friendship:
Jon embodied loud, vocal leadership, while I preferred to lead quietly by example. Jon envisioned bold changes; I felt content with the way things were.

We seemed opposites in many respects, but our friendship began because of Jon's warm, outgoing character. He took the initiative to reach out and make friends with others. I became friends with Jon because of his remarkable ability to welcome outsiders into his friendship.

While we were in high school, I had a unique experience that offered a glimpse into Jon's future. I invited him to meet at my house for a distance run on a Sunday afternoon. After the run, he wanted to know what I was doing that afternoon. I told him that I was going to Sunday night Mass. Jon said he wanted to come along. Surprised by this, I asked if he was serious. To most high schoolers, going to church was an activity done as part of a routine or enforced by their parents. Adding to my concern was the fact that Jon was not a Roman Catholic. But he assured me that he really wanted to go to church with me.

So my mom and I attended Mass with Jon as our guest. He appeared at home there. He truly enjoyed himself and sang the hymns louder and with much more energy than everyone around him.

He seemed excited to take it all in, to see how our faith was similar and different to his. This was a strong indicator to me that Jon's future would be based on sharing his faith with others.

Through our college years, I was able to see other examples of Jon putting his faith into action. It was inspiring for me to see this person who got such satisfaction and happiness from helping others, while most of my peers only received that satisfaction through their own personal gain. Most people in their twenties keep busy taking care of themselves, but Jon actually thought about taking care of others.

I often got postcards, handwritten letters, and emails from Jon, wherever he was, sometimes in the Western US or South America. He always told interesting stories about his religious service and youth ministry, mostly happy stories. He did face some tough times, but he always remained positive and found some humor in the situation. Jon inspired me to keep in contact with my other friends. He always ended with, "Peace & Love, Jon," a closing message that no one else I knew ever used. But it was a message that Jon exemplified better than anyone else."

Jon's best friend and running partner at Augustana College was a journalism major from Sioux City, Iowa. Mike's parents became our good friends as we traveled the running circuit together. We often joked that Jon and Mike could spend hours together without saying a word, yet enjoy the experience.

On Mike's twenty-second birthday, he was a little ornery because he had to get up for a 6:30 a.m. track workout. In came Jon wearing a homemade party hat, carrying cupcakes he had baked, and singing "Happy Birthday" to Mike.

Wired to Love

Jon's high school friend Alexis (Alex) is like another daughter to Linda and me. When I asked her to write about what Jon meant to her, she described Jon as an "athlete of love." I was moved by her connecting his passion for running with his capacity to love. I saw that Jon was wired to run. Alex confirmed that he was also wired to love.

Alexis wrote:

Jon's running was impenetrable to me as much as I sought to participate in and offer support to him. I have grown to see his athleticism not so much as an isolated and extraordinary gift, but rather as an extension or manifestation of his character. He poured out discipline, hard work, patience, persistence, hope, and grace into many areas of his life, especially his relationships. Jon stepped into our house with a sense of grace and courage, with his lighthearted playfulness as he jumped on my brother's back, told silly and absurd jokes, danced through our kitchen to his own music, and simply laughed out loud. Jon poured and oozed and hugged the love of God onto us with kindness and gentleness. He was a pastor, a healer, a friend, and a kind of athlete of love to us. I don't think I have ever loved or been more fully loved by anyone.

We found Jon's tattered road atlas in his car in July 2006. He had marked the thirty-five states where he had either competed or trained. I will forever cherish those years—often in extreme cold, rain, heat, and humidity—watching Jon run with passion and joy. Jon's legs were kissed by God. To Jon Francis, hiking, running, and climbing provided a special and unique experience—a spiritual bond with nature that was inherent to Jon's lifelong faith journey.

Just before he graduated from high school, Jon found a Christian college that excited him. Augustana is a small Lutheran College located in Sioux Falls, South Dakota. Jon worked tirelessly at Augustana to understand his faith and to live it through his works. He was active in Habitat for Humanity and Campus Crusade for Christ. At the same time, he was a Bible Study leader and a mentor to Hispanic children for Lutheran Social Services and the Sioux Falls School District.

He wrote a short story in college that captured his love for God's creation. He described a small lake and its path near his boyhood home:

"Make connections; let rip . . ."
by Jon Francis (2004)

I borrowed a quote from Annie Dillard's *Pilgrim at Tinker Creek*: "Make connections, let rip; and dance where you can."

I let rip with joy when I quietly peruse the contents of the forest floor. I break forth when I shout from a mountain peak after climbing to the top.

My bursting forth takes the form of celebration, of grace, of awe and wonder, of humility and of thanksgiving. I am celebrating the goodness of nature. I am thankful for the goodness of the created world.

I do not know why, but I am closer to God when I am outside.

Little Carnelian Lake lies, as the crow flies, 500 meters from my front door. The sandy beach, located lakeshore at the end of the township park is half a mile by foot away from my house.

There is trail made of sand, dirt, and gravel that winds its way through the woods to the lakeshore. This trail, the lake, and the park all constitute together my favorite place.

Countless times, I have asked, what would I do without that lake and little patch of woods? Between the gravel parking lot and the small sandy beach is my haven and my refuge.

I do not remain silent. I give glory to God for her abundant creation. There is goodness all round. There is goodness deep within.

Linda and I always wanted Jon to come home during his summer breaks from college to be with us, but Jon felt he needed to do more to help pay his way. In 2001 Jon, age nineteen, applied for a summer counselor position with Luther Heights Bible Camp, near Ketchum, Idaho. I found this application letter on Jon's computer:

My qualifications for being a counselor include being a leader at two Teens Encounter Christ weekends and being involved in three other weekends. In early high school, I volunteered for two weeks at

Gethsemane Day Camp in Minneapolis. I have been a delegate and on a youth panel at the annual convention for the Episcopal Church of Minnesota. I was a peer counselor at Stillwater High School as well as a Track and Cross Country captain.

From 1998 to 2000, I taught Sunday school at Ascension Episcopal, and during the summer of 2000, I was a "nanny" for two elementary (school) age boys. Presently, I am a mentor at Edison Middle School in Sioux Falls and helping plan a retreat for college Christians.

There are many people who have influenced my faith journey. Primarily there are my parents, who raised me in a Christian home and exposed me to a Christian lifestyle. My parents gave me the tools that have allowed me to enter into Christianity. Another large influence was my youth leader, Rev. LeeAnne Watkins. She sparked my interest and desire to find community and to take further steps toward Christianity.

I became involved in youth group, community service, and youth ministries all because of LeeAnne. She helped shape my young, but unfortunately immature, faith. She was honest, loving, and open to us. She helped me invite myself and put down my roots into a religious life.

A lot of my friends from the Teens Encounter Christ program have made a large impact on my life. My friends Nick, Katrina, Amanda, and Kelsey have all made my life better. I am still friends with all of them, and we converse and meet each other year after year. These four especially taught me how to love excitedly, and how to be a friend.

We are all in separate places right now, but I will never forget how they've cared for me. I turn to these friends still in my times of deep questioning, worry, disappointment, and joy. I trust and love all of them more because we shared a part of God together. These friends still excite and encourage me. I continue in my faith because each of these people has shared a part of their faith, in various forms, with me.

I began some deep questioning of Christianity at the end of my senior year of high school. After a year of mulling over these questions, I found myself in a completely different situation. I didn't have a will, a mind, a faith, or a life that fit together for Christianity anymore. I moved away, pushed away, and held at arm's length skepticism about the life that I had before.

I do not think that I would ever be able to claim a real and significant faith if I had not gone through my period of deep reckoning. Our pastor, Paul Rohde, at Augustana tells me that a questioning faith is seen as more real than a blind following faith. I tend to believe him.

My close friend Alexis helped push along my deep questions and doubts about Christianity. My world view and mind-set were changed by her ideas. Alexis had become a passionate and dedicated Christian. In time, she encouraged my journey toward a new formation of faith. Alexis and I discuss our faith life weekly and still share our lives together."

Jon, a religion major in college, often questioned theology. The chaplain at Augustana assured Jon that a "questioning faith is a genuine faith."

During his time of questioning, Jon wrote this universal lament:

Does God Ever Intervene Anymore?

by Jon Francis

I know that God may be around, but I don't understand why things are a certain way. Why couldn't the earth, life, be different? It is not the best of all possible worlds. Is it our life as humans to keep failing with our responsibility?

I grow tired of failing. I grow tired of trying. It does seem like I may never do enough. Does God ever intervene anymore?

I believe that we should question God if we do not fully understand. But I am not fully sure about what my questioning and thinking has done for me. Why is God not trustworthy?

Is it only our own fault because of the way we've made the world? The dance and the circle of questions continue. I feel a sense of injustice, uncertainty, and a longing to reach points of resolution.

If we keep demanding that God yield up His answers, perhaps someday we will understand them. And then we shall be something more than clever apes, and we shall dance with God.

I will walk the middle path. There is a time to question and a time of assurance. I will walk the questioning path, and I will walk the listening, praying, and receiving paths, as well.

Sometime during his final year of college, Jon called on the phone to say, "Dad, I've decided to become a Lutheran." Linda and I had seen the process evolving over the years. We knew that raising a child in

Minnesota and sending him off to a Lutheran College probably meant an eventual conversion to Lutheranism.

"Why?" I asked. Jon responded that he was excited about the youth ministry that the Evangelical Lutheran Church in America (ELCA) was doing, and he wanted to be part of it.

"Jon, you'll still be a Christian; won't you?" I teased. He assured me that he would.

I remained in awe of my son's ability to maintain a 3.5 grade point average through college, compete in Division II Athletics, hold a part-time campus job, and participate in a significant ministry in the community. Jon had been on the five-year plan, earning majors in religion, Spanish, and international studies. Due to his earned scholarships and his campus and summer jobs, Jon left college with no student loans. In his fifth year of eligibility, he voluntarily gave up his athletic scholarship, so his coach could use the money to attract fresh talent.

Jon's sister Melissa and niece Katie went with us to Jon's graduation ceremony in South Dakota in May 2005. He was the only graduate to wear "Thanks Mom and Dad" taped to the top of his cap. He wore flip-flops and shorts under his gown. Jon's sense of fun and commitment to diversity added to Augustana's student culture. When we attended a reception at the home of the college president, Dr. Halverson expressed genuine affection and respect for Jon and his contributions to campus life.

During his college semester abroad in Guatemala, Jon had worked at an orphanage, willing to do whatever the job called for, helping the kids or shoveling pig manure. Jon showed maturity, leadership, and a responsible work ethic in every position he filled—team captain, leader at TEC, camp counselor—and as a dishwasher during high school.

I didn't really need to worry, but I was still a little concerned, after his five years of college, about Jon's preparation for the "real" world. During the summer of 2005, he had interviewed over the phone for the part-time youth director position in Ogden, Utah. Ascension Lutheran Church couldn't afford to fill a full-time position. I later learned that Jon "blew away" the interviewers. He went to work in Utah in the fall of 2005. Since the position was without benefits, Jon found a second job at the Weber County Library.

We were able to read about Jon's youth group activities in the Ascension Lutheran newsletter. We heard more by phone as he described the difficulties of gaining the trust of teenagers and trying to develop a Christian community.

Jon spent that Christmas with his sister, Jocelyn, in California. He wanted to be in a warm place to run as well as spend time with his two-year-old niece, Audrey, and meet his six-month-old nephew, Charlie.

Jon promised to be home in Minnesota for his twenty-fourth birthday in March 2006 and to help us pack up the house. Linda and I were moving into a townhouse in Stillwater. I called it "assisted living." Someone else would now cut the grass and shovel the snow. I could sell my lawnmower, wheelbarrow, and yard tools.

As promised, Jon came home for his birthday. He quietly packed up his bedroom and most of his carefully kept athletic equipment, well-maintained toys such as matchbox cars, action figures, and Legos. I sensed that he was upset that we were selling his boyhood home, but we never talked about it.

One of my happiest memories is our dinner conversation when I turned to him and said, "Jon, when I get to heaven, I'm going to ask God why *She* didn't do a better job in creation. Why is our world so full of suffering, chaos, tribal warfare, and violence?"

Jon thought for a minute, as he often did, and responded, "Dad, isn't that kind of arrogant?"

"Perhaps," I quickly said, "but I think I deserve to know. And by the way, if there is no heaven, I'm really going to be mad!"

Jon's boss, Laura, at Luther Heights shared her memories of Jon. She talked about his sense of fun and how good he was with the kids—dancing, singing—his ability to reach even the toughest kids.

Laura described how warmly Jon greeted her when he came back to the Luther Heights that last summer (2006):

He moved differently, looked different to me somehow. It became apparent to me within that first day that he found his stride. He was comfortable in his own skin. He had come into his own. There was a new confidence in the way he spoke, the way he moved, how he shared with others who he was and what he believed. It was a marvelous thing to see—he felt so new to me, yet he was still the Jon I had known all along—intensely curious about religion, his life of faith, the world, and the big questions that involve all of those elements and many more. Over the years we had enjoyed many conversations on these topics.

I was excited to hear him talk about his potential next moves in ministry, including seminary somewhere in his future. He never knew that I would begin study at Luther Seminary in St. Paul, Minnesota, after that summer. I waited until the end of the summer to tell the staff so that my leaving wouldn't be a distraction to the lives of staff and campers. I am sad that we did not get to talk about our common passion that had us both eyeing ordained ministry. —Laura

I have been moved to passionately adore and often idealize my son. I was nearly two generations older than Jon, and often I could barely believe that he genuinely wanted to spend time with me. I missed so much of his brief life. When Jon was growing up, I worked too many hours, made too many trips away from home, and said, "Yes" too many times to activities that took me away from my family.

I now remember with painful regret many missed opportunities to spend time with my son, to play games, build things, just sit quietly together, or camp under the stars. I didn't visit Jon in Guatemala, in Utah, or in Idaho. I didn't share Jon's love for the mountains, and we never did a western "road trip" together. If only I could have a do over.

It's a nagging regret that I remember having only one discussion about theology with Jon. I should have asked him to explain the Holy Trinity to me. It would have been fascinating to hear my son describe this complex Christian concept.

I will hold in my heart forever the last words Jon and I spoke. In the summer of 2006, he returned to Luther Heights Bible Camp.

He called me in the evening of Wednesday, July 12, 2006. Once again, he was having a great time at camp, but thought it was probably his last summer in Idaho. Jon said he knew it was hard for us to be so far from him, but he loved the mountains, living out west, and his work as a youth minister.

"That's okay, son," I said. "It's called leaving home. We all leave home."

Jon said he needed to go, to prepare for the next day at camp. We said, "Goodbye," and "I love you."

That was the last time I ever spoke with my son.

"Jonathan . . . greatly beloved were you to me; your love to me was wonderful . . ." 2 Samuel 1:26

A Celebration of Life

For the rest of the summer of 2006, people asked about our plans for a funeral service for Jon, a chance to join as a community and pay their respects to him. But didn't a funeral require a body? I would never again hug Jon's lean, athletic body, kiss his handsome face, or smell his distinctive scent. Jon was lost, and we couldn't find him. Maybe we never would. My confidence was fading that we could ever bring him home. So we planned a memorial service.

Working with our priest, Father Jerry, we hoped to create a celebration that reflected the love and joy Jon brought into the lives of all who knew him and to honor Jon's commitment to share his faith as a teacher and a friend.

On Saturday, September 9, we held a "Celebration of the Life and Ministry of Jon Francis" at Ascension Episcopal Church in Stillwater, the church where Jon grew up and the church that nurtured the formation of his faith. The day before the service, I stood in the pulpit and practiced reading Jon's eulogy six times before I was able to get through it without crying.

Our three daughters and five grandchildren sat in the front pew alongside Linda and me as the celebration began. Jocelyn wore Jon's purple high school prom tuxedo in tribute. Family and dear friends came to Minnesota from across the country along with Jon's teammates, coaches, classmates from high school and college, and friends from Luther Heights Camp. Jon's high school sweetheart, Alexis, and her family sat with us. We were surrounded in love by more than five-hundred mourners—friends from Ascension Church in Stillwater, relatives, neighbors, and many friends from community, politics, and business.

I stood in the pulpit and spoke.

A Eulogy for My Son Jon

We should not be here today. This should not be happening to us. Children should bury their parents.

But we ARE HERE today to celebrate the brief life and ministry of Jon Francis. We thank you for gathering to remember our son, mourn his loss, and celebrate his life.

Since my family and I began our journey of sorrow many weeks ago, dozens of people have spoken to us and said, "You raised an awesome son." Jon touched us. Jon was a man of strong character, deep faith, humility, patience, fun, adventure, and unconditional love.

I have thanked so many people for their kind words and responded, "His mother did a fine job, didn't she?" Jon's mother, Linda, and I fell in love many years ago. And we often spoke about a time when we would be married, have children together, and raise a family.

In high school, we picked out our children's names. We agreed that our firstborn son would be named Jonathan David Francis. Jonathan and David, two strong Old Testament names. I remembered from my Sunday school days that Jonathan loved David. (I Samuel: 18) "And it came to pass . . . that the soul of Jonathan was knit with the soul of David, and Jonathan loved him as his own soul."

A part of my soul was torn away, leaving a hole in my heart and a big void in my family.

Since July 15 I have learned a great deal about mountain search and rescue, and about grief and loss. Here are some things I have learned:

The loss of a child is the deepest and most long-lasting sorrow known to humanity. We've not only lost our son, but also his future. We've lost not only Jon's physical body, but also his dreams, his accomplishments. I cannot ignore, avoid, or go around the sorrow of my loss. I have to work through it. Help me in my grief. Tell me stories about Jon. Don't ask me questions I can't answer.

Whatever happened on that mountain was not God's will. It was a terrible and tragic accident. God does not will death. God wants us to live. I believe that God shares our sorrow today. God's promise of

Eternal Life is wonderful. But today I would rather have the promise of hugging my son on his twenty-fifth birthday.

Closure is a myth. Closure is for bank accounts—not for love accounts. I know I will have a love account with Jon my entire life.

Our son Jon was patient. For six years, he patiently put up with me as his soccer coach.

When Jon was fourteen he said, "Dad, you're going to retire next year, right?" I said, "Yes, Jon, it's time for me to retire."

Our son Jon was humble. When he was a sophomore in high school, he ran varsity cross -country. His team had an awesome year. They were undefeated, won the state championship, and were voted national champion high school boys cross country team. When Jostens created a super-bowl-style ring for the team, Jon would not order a ring. When we encouraged him to buy one, Jon said, "Dad, I don't need a ring. I know what we did." Touching his heart, he said, "I carry it in here."

Our son Jon was a man of deep faith. Jon's faith formation was supported by this church, its strong youth ministry, and Jon's experience in Teens Encounter Christ. When Jon was in high school, he and the Ascension Youth Group worked at a homeless shelter for children in Minneapolis. Many of the children were abandoned and abused. At the end of the service week, our priest came to us and said, "Your son Jon has a real gift for ministry to children." We were pleased to see Jon live his ministry through high school, college, and after graduation.

When we stopped to gather Jon's belongings at Ascension Lutheran church in Ogden, where Jon was youth director, many members thanked us and told us how Jon had touched their lives. I asked several people how he did in his first job out of college. They said Jon was awesome. He was a blessing and a gift.

His mentor at Ascension, Pastor David Kiel, told me that Jon had a down-to-earth, genuine ministry. He met the kids where they were and brought fun and joy to his ministry. He attracted others by living an authentic, faith-filled life.

When my family and our friend, Father Jerry, gathered at the base of the mountain in Idaho that Jon had climbed, Jon's sisters reminded us that Jon found a way to live above the pride and pettiness that afflict many of us. Jon was seldom mean-spirited, complaining, or petty. Jon seemed to see the best in everyone.

Jon *got* it! He loved life. And he loved people. He loved deeply and was deeply loved.

Jon knew that we were not placed on earth to grab all of the objects, money, and status we can. We are born into this world to make a difference, to love God, and to love and serve others.

Jon *got* it! I believe in my heart that Jon saw the world as God's wonderful creation. And the beautiful, natural world that God created cried out for protection and preservation. Jon saw all of the creatures in the world as God's creatures, worthy of respect. And Jon saw *all people* as God's children, worthy of unconditional love. That is how Jon Francis lived his life.

I know that Jon ran long distances and climbed mountains to challenge himself; but more importantly, he did those things to glorify God. Climbing mountains was a spiritual experience for him. I know Jon felt close to God at the summit. He left a note in the summit registry on the Grand Mogul that read: "07/15/06. Jon Francis, LHBC [Luther Heights Bible Camp] and Ogden, Utah. Climbed avalanche field to east face and east ridge. Great times bouldering! All Glory to God for the climb and the beautiful Sawtooths."

Jon called home the week before he climbed the Grand Mogul. That was the last time I spoke with my son. He said, "Dad, I know you would like me to be in Minnesota and closer to home, but my ministry is out here."

I said, "Jon, I know. It's called leaving home. It's all right. We all leave home.'"

I am grateful to God that I was given the opportunity to give my son my blessing, and to say to him, "It's all right, son. It's called leaving home."

Finally, I am most grateful to God for giving us such a remarkable son—for giving us the gift of Jon.

Linda and I thanked everyone for coming and for remembering Jon. We were profoundly touched by those whose lives had been touched by our son. At a time when I felt abandoned by God, I saw God in the faces of the hundreds of others who encircled us to help us bear our suffering.

Jon Francis on the summit of Thompson Peak, Sawtooth Mountains, Idaho

CHAPTER 3

GOOD GRIEF?

"Be gracious to me, O LORD, for I am in distress; my eye wastes away from grief, my soul and body also. For my life is spent with sorrow, and my years with sighing; my strength fails because of my misery, and my bones waste away." Psalm 31:9–10

What is Grief?

While I was planning, organizing, and participating in our search and recovery efforts, Linda started to read books about grief and loss. She was reading *Ambiguous Loss: Learning to Live with Unresolved Grief,* written by Dr. Pauline Boss, a professor at the University of Minnesota and an expert and author on "ambiguous loss"—often called unresolved loss. Linda came to me and said, "David. There is a name for our grief. It's called unresolved loss."

Unresolved loss, not knowing where your loved one is or what happened, piles grief upon grief.

Dr. Boss writes, "Ambiguous loss is distressful and can lead to depressive episodes, physical illnesses, emotional upheaval, and family conflict."

Years later, when I met Dr. Boss, she told me that as a military officer I was understandably trained to seek mastery or control over any urgent situation. She was right. Being out of control is an unnatural act for me. Consequently, it is not surprising that I approached my debilitating grief with a "can do" attitude. I was driven to research, understand, cope, overcome, and "master" my grief. I wanted to be a victor, not a victim. *Show me the SOP! Where is the STANDARD OPERATING PROCEDURE that will guide me through this? I can take this hill! I can achieve this mission!*

I embarked on a mission to learn as much as I could. First I learned that when a loved one is lost, we don't just lose their presence, we also lose their future—particularly their future with us. I felt that acutely. Our lives and our futures are forever altered. I also learned that it is widely understood that the death of a child (flesh of our flesh) is considered the greatest suffering known to humanity. I can confirm that it is certainly the greatest suffering I have ever known.

I have two bookshelves full of books on grief and loss. Medical doctors, psychiatrists, psychologists, and professors wrote many of them. Though they are often clinical and scientific studies, tedious and impersonal, I found much of their information helpful to me.

In *Grief Counseling and Grief Therapy: A Handbook for the Mental Health Practitioner* by J. William Worden, PhD, the author talks about normal human behavior and our need to form attachments with significant others throughout our lives in order to meet many of our physical and psychological needs. As children we rely on our parents and families to provide for our safety, survival, and nurturing. If it is absent, we experience deprivation. We live in a complex society and we must rely on others, particularly our significant others, to fulfill our human attachment needs. When an attachment is lost, we are deprived, and we mourn our loss.

Grief is a noun that means deep sorrow. Some synonyms are: misery, sadness, heartache, heartbreak, anguish, despair, desolation, distress, agony, torment, affliction, suffering, woe, dejection, etc. Even reading those words caused me pain. Grief is a natural reaction to loss and a universal and a personal experience.

Worden tells us that grief is a strong, sometimes overwhelming emotion. Each person's experience is influenced by the nature of the loss—the death of a loved one or the terminal diagnosis of self or loved one, the end of an important relationship, job loss, loss of independence due to disability, etc. Regardless of the specific loss, the synonyms for grief are the result. Grief can leave a person feeling numb and removed from daily life and unable to engage in their regular activities or daily responsibilities.

Russell Friedman and John James in *Grief Recovery Handbook: The Action Program for Moving Beyond Death, Divorce, and Other Losses* discuss the many causes of grief other than that of a loved one's death. They stress that grief is natural and normal as a response to any kind of loss. As the most powerful of all emotions, grief is also the most neglected and misunderstood experience—by those grieving as well as those in their company.

Getting Stuck (or maybe not even getting started)

Grieving is work—hard, painful work. And embarking on a journey of healing is optional, not mandatory. We can choose to do our grief work or not. Grief is such a complex and strong emotion that I never fail to be surprised by how unique and personal the experience is for each person. On my grief journey, I have met some grief sufferers who are not moving forward. They have not yet actually become grief "travelers." They are content or willing to stay where they are. They are, in fact, stuck. For countless reasons, they are unable to gather the emotional strength and support, the determination, motivation, or the guidance to walk through the valley. To do so requires effort, courage, and work.

Psychiatrist Erich Lindemann, a pioneer is the study of grief, coined the term "grief work" in 1944 to describe the tasks we must complete in order to resolve our grief. In speaking with other grief travelers, I found there is some agreement.

Throughout my journey, I have become a believer in the importance of understanding the emotional stages of grieving. Grieving is a personal process that has no time limit and no one "right" way to do it. We all seem to grieve at our own pace. And it is common to repeat and revisit the stages and steps.

In a meeting with a Lutheran pastor who invited me to speak at his church, he asked, "David, what are your takeaways? What have you learned since the death of your son?"

I struggled to answer him. Many of my responses are in this book.

"Normal" Grief

One of many books I've read since Jon's death is *On Death and Dying,* by a Swiss psychiatrist, Elisabeth Kübler-Ross, published in 1969. Dr. Kübler-Ross conducted a pioneering clinical study wherein she recorded the psychological stages of terminally ill (dying) people. Her book is an important and helpful book for anyone confronted with terminal illness and can use some help framing and identifying the associated complex feelings.

Kübler-Ross is credited with advances in the care of dying patients and their families and the creation of the concept of a hospice program to support those who are nearing death. Toward the end of her book, she discusses similarities between terminally ill people and surviving victims as she describes five stages of "normal" grief. All five are completely normal reactions to a horrific reality.

The first stage is *denial.* A first reaction to finding out about the terminal illness or a death of a loved one is to not believe it—to deny the reality of this terrible news. This type of defense mechanism helps us deal with the harshness of a grim reality. We may even find it hard to absorb the shocking facts surrounding the news. This type of reaction has a way of helping us "mask" our pain.

The second stage is *anger.* As the pain becomes sharper and its true reality is undeniable and we try to redirect our intense emotional feelings about the "unfairness" of the situation, the result is anger and rage. We might lash out in anger and resentment even at those we love, the person who is dying, or even one who has already died—the person who caused our deep pain by leaving us. These emotions are so strong, and we know they are often irrational, that we may also feel guilty for experiencing them.

The third stage is *bargaining*. As we feel helpless and vulnerable, we may try to "make a deal" with God to alter or postpone the outcome in exchange for being a better person—or some other trade. This is the stage of "If only" regrets. I lamented, *If only I had known Jon was climbing tall mountains alone.*

The fourth stage is *depression*. The main features are the profound sadness and regret at the loss that can permeate all aspects of everyday life and also include guilt and shame. Another part is much more internal and private as we prepare for the separation and find ways to say goodbye to the loved one.

The fifth and final stage is *acceptance* of what is happening and coming to terms with the loss. This is the hardest one to accomplish in my experience. This stage can also be associated with withdrawal for a time and perhaps a period of calmness. We may resist any form of acceptance or feel we don't deserve to feel any peace.

Many people do not experience the five stages in the order listed here, nor do they need to. We may experience each stage with different levels of intensity. If a death is sudden and unexpected, the denial and anger stages can last a long time or perhaps never be overcome. Although there has been some debate over the years about stages and steps of grief, my own personal journey of grief traveled through several of these steps.

I agree with Kübler-Ross that we must allow ourselves to feel grief as it comes over us. Avoiding or resisting our feelings will only prolong the natural healing process. But others can be there for us and help comfort us through this process.

My Grief Journey

Granger E. Westberg, a chaplain and professor at the University of Chicago Divinity School and Medical School, turned a powerful sermon into a small, but amazing book, *Good Grief: A Companion for Every Loss*, in 1979. His book was updated and celebrated in a new edition fifty years later. Similar to Kübler-Ross, Westberg described stages of grief, all of which I identified with in my personal grief journey. He lists ten stages that closely parallel hers: shock, emotion, depression, physical distress, panic, guilt, anger, resistance, hope, and acceptance.

The first, *shock*, Westberg called "a blessing" because our sorrow triggers a temporary escape from the pain, clouding our thinking and shielding us from the harsh reality. My shock prevented me from confronting the Idaho authorities about their unfairness, dereliction of duty, and their quick abandonment of the search for Jon.

I remained silent when the incident commander again said, "David, it's time to give your son up to the mountain." I was immobilized by disbelief. I was stunned and paralyzed by a feeling of helplessness. When we begin to be able to express our pain as that shock dissipates— we have "an uncontrollable urge" to cry out. This emotional release, in my experience, is the beginning of our grief work. Studies have shown that the tears of grief are different and more powerful than normal wetting tears. This is when we are able to speak about our loss and even ask others to grieve with us. If others can't or won't listen to us, we feel isolated in our pain. We can feel entirely alone. Westberg called this a feeling of being "enclosed in darkness" or deep despair.

The sense that no one understands the depth of our pain can continue after the funeral when the rest of the world goes on with life, and we don't know how to do so. This is a feeling of abandonment that often leads to depression. We need help to climb out of this serious illness. Depression is a disease that requires medical intervention.

Grief counseling, support groups, and the understanding of friends, family, and others are all important for recovery from emotional distress. Many do not realize that the internalized pain of grief can also be the cause of physical illness and pain. Some sufferers may even question their own sanity. The confusion and inability to think straight can cause a person to panic and feel further out of control. Knowing that these feelings are all part of a normal grief process, and that it is possible to work through such feelings, are important for gaining a better sense of control.

Westberg highlighted the significant role of guilt in bereavement as "one of the strongest emotions humans can feel." We ruminate over the all the interactions we had—especially unpleasant exchanges with our loved one, anything cruel or thoughtless that we may have said or done. Grief travelers may feel guilty and responsible for the loss—the source of the "if only."

If only I had . . . If only I had done . . . If only I had known . . .

This is entirely normal and expected.

As parents, we undoubtedly feel a desire, obligation, and yearning to protect our children from harm. When our children are hurt, or worse, we naturally feel guilt and have a sense of failed responsibility for being unable to prevent the harm or death.

I was devastated by my guilt. I was overcome with regret about all of the things I did not do with my son when he was alive. In addition, I was bereft that I did not know about his risk-taking and did not intervene. I felt responsible, as though I should have known.

To help cope with my guilt, I followed the advice of a more mature grief traveler who wrote a letter to his dead child.

So I wrote a letter to my son.

Dear Jon,

You were with us for such a short time. How I miss you. You made my life whole. I loved you beyond measure. Your brief life and your remarkable qualities are now an inspiration to me.

I reminded Jon that he was not perfect.

But you were human. You were often stubborn, impatient, and ornery. Sometimes you were testy and unapproachable, particularly when you were going deep before a competitive running event. During those times, we dared not talk to you. Sometimes you reduced your mother to tears with your grumpy attitude.

I remember when you were in college and developed a persistent hamstring injury. Your running performance and speed declined, and your frustration and post-race grumpiness increased. My heart ached for you.

I thought about how often he took on difficult challenges.

I know you were close to God in the wilderness. I didn't know you were climbing rugged mountains—alone. Did you know how risky that was? You always had confidence in your ability to accomplish tough goals—a notable strength of yours, and perhaps (literally) your fatal flaw.

But still, he was extraordinary.

In my heart of hearts, when I remember your remarkable life, I am content to idealize you. You earned it. I often saw you change sadness into joy. You were with us for only a fleeting moment. But in that time, you made a difference. You were a gift to us from God.

Love, Dad

Westberg stresses that blame, of ourselves ("if only") or of others, is the natural side effect of our need to understand our loss. We naturally become "highly critical of everything and everyone" who may have been associated with the loss. Trauma victims often blame themselves, and/or we become angry at our deceased loved ones for whatever they may have done that caused our loss.

In the event of a child's death, other parents may be likely to avoid the parents of the dead child. Those bereaved parents represent their worst fears.

Family relations can be disrupted and strained over so many

things—funeral arrangements, distribution of personal belongings or items of special endearment, or maybe resentment about who "didn't care enough" to call or show up at key points. Arguments may break out over who has the deepest grief, who has the right to talk, and who needs to be an active and compassionate listener.

As others return to normal life, we may resent that *they* are able to move on—that they do not understand the depth of our loss. We may then resist returning to any type of normalcy in our own lives and become "comfortable" in our grief. I found this the most difficult and most long-lasting stage for me, which included my anger at God. "God sits in His heaven and does nothing."

This anger was one of the motivators that led me several months later to create the Jon Francis Foundation. Our mission would be to honor Jon's memory and to bring some good from his loss. This was a way to keep Jon's memory alive and help other people who experienced similar tragedies.

I heeded Westberg's warning that becoming "stuck" in grief will delay healing and cause continuing mental and physical distress. He stresses that we must remember that there is hope. The grief and faith work, counseling as needed, along with the support and affection of our friends and family, plus "time" will slowly restore our hope. He reminds us, "We are changed. Life will never be the same. However, we begin to realize that we need not fear life. We can live it again. We can even love it again. Not everything has been taken from us. Life can be affirmed."

Takeaways

Grief is a powerful emotion of deep sorrow. Synonyms include misery, sadness, heartache, heartbreak, anguish, despair, desolation, distress, agony, torment, affliction, suffering, woe, dejection, etc.

Grief has no timetable and no "right way" to move forward, but healing is possible.

Let yourself feel your feelings and let others help to comfort you.

Consider some widely recommended paths for providing comfort and healing grief such as conducting and/or participating in dedicated rituals, creating memorials, writing about the loss and the loved one, and/or adopting causes on behalf of the loved one.

Consider whether your grief may feel familiar along Kübler-Ross's five stages of "normal" grief: denial, anger, bargaining, depression, and acceptance.

Consider Westberg's stages of Good Grief.

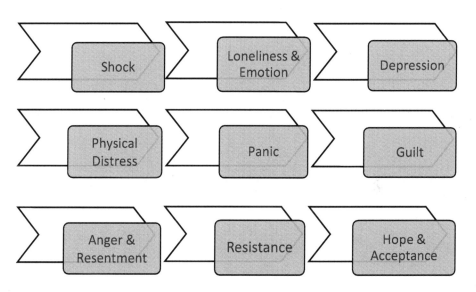

PART II

TRAVELING THROUGH
THE VALLEY

CHAPTER 4

SORROW, DEPRESSION, DESPAIR
WHY DOES IT HURT SO MUCH?

"How is faith to endure, O God, when you allow all this scraping and tearing on us? You have allowed rivers of blood to flow, mountains of suffering to pile up, sobs to become humanity's song . . ."

—Professor Nicholas Wolterstorff, *Lament for a Son*

We returned home after our unsuccessful searches for Jon in August 2006 to a tall pile of mail. I found that more than one friend had sent me a copy of *Lament for a Son* written by Nicholas Wolterstorff, professor of theology at Yale Divinity School. Professor Wolterstorff's twenty-five-year-old son, Eric, died while mountain climbing alone in Austria. Along with a sympathy card, one copy was mailed from Spokane, Washington, by Bishop Martin Wells, Jon's bishop.

I opened the book and read: "The call came at 3:30 on that Sunday afternoon, a bright sunny day." I closed the book. I couldn't keep going. *No!* This couldn't be. Our call came at 3:15 on a Sunday afternoon, a bright and sunny day.

Lament sat at my bedside for many days until I was able to open it again. When I did, I read, "There's a hole in the world now. In the place where he was, there's now just nothing . . . The world is emptier. My son is gone. Only a hole remains, a void, a gap, never to be filled."

While reading *Lament for a Son,* I felt a small sense of comfort. Someone else felt the same unbearable pain I was feeling and was able to express it. Someone else experienced the agony of losing a young son. Another person—another man, another father—had experienced the same desolation as I and found a way to give voice to his and my distress. *Lament* is a beautiful love song from a father to his son who died too soon, too sadly, and too suddenly.

Traumatic Loss

I joined Nicholas in traumatic grief. What can anyone who is a victim of traumatic grief expect?

I am a retired US Navy nuclear submarine officer. I was trained to take charge in an emergency and quickly assess and solve difficult problems. But on the evening of July 17, 2006, I sat paralyzed by my sorrow —feeling helpless and hopeless.

Why was I paralyzed? I later learned in therapy that I was operating from the fear center of my brain—the amygdala. I was reduced to reptilian behavior and thinking. This was the beginning of several weeks of my primitive thinking. Because of the massive trauma, the deep, heartbreaking, mental injury caused by the loss of my son, my brain chemistry was out of whack. Trauma messes with the brain.

Trauma is an injury or wound to living tissue caused by an outside agent—a disordered psychic or behavioral state of mind that results from severe mental or emotional stress or physical injury. Such emotional upset can cause the brain to react in fight, flight, or freeze modes. A person might become angry, volatile, and aggressive or perhaps become passive and withdrawn. Anyone who has raised teenagers knows the impact of chemical/hormone changes on the brain.

Traumatic events can alter the brain's chemistry and trigger acute stress disorder (ASD) or posttraumatic stress disorder (PTSD) that spurs further confusion, anger, anxiety, difficulty or inability to control emotions, fear, sadness, and/or shame. PTSD, once called shell shock or battle fatigue syndrome, is a serious condition that can develop after a person has experienced or witnessed a traumatic or terrifying event in which serious physical harm or threat occurred (like a warrior in battle).

In shock at losing Jon, I was overwhelmed. When my amygdala became engaged and my choice was fight, flight, or freeze, my brain chose freeze. I was numb.

That first week in Idaho, the Francis family and Jon's friends did not receive attention or care from any victim's advocate. We were ignored, isolated, and kept in the dark like mushrooms. My brain was flooded with a stress hormone (cortisol). I was full of fear. I had no hope. This "brain knowledge" became important to me in two ways:

1. My ability to heal from traumatic grief, and
2. The work of the Jon Francis Foundation required that I understand and be sensitive to the behavior of other trauma victims who we would try to help.

I later learned in therapy that I suffered from both depression and posttraumatic stress disorder after losing Jon—a common result of intense brain trauma. Depression is an extremely complex disease. No one knows exactly what causes it, but it can occur for a variety of reasons. Some people experience depression during a serious medical illness. For others depression may be triggered by life changes such as a move or the death of a loved one. Still others have a family history of depression.

I have suffered and recovered from two bouts of depression. The first was brought on many years before by a combination of intense corporate workplace stress and an abusive manager. When in a business meeting, I was unable to follow the conversation or understand what was decided. I felt panic. The experience was frightening and still vivid in my memory. At the time, Jon was nine, and Linda and I were engaged in family therapy to help navigate life with three teenage daughters. I described my symptoms to our family counselor: feeling sad, lack of energy, trouble sleeping, fatigue, and difficulty thinking, concentrating, and making decisions. The therapist told me I had classic symptoms of clinical depression. I received the help I needed right away—both the medical intervention and the talk therapy.

When this second bout with depression came after Jon went missing in Idaho, I recognized the feeling, and I knew what was happening with my brain. I could see that I was irritable and angry. I was emotionally cut off and detached from my family and all others who were not supporters of my pain and purpose. I felt jumpy and constantly on guard and often revisited the accident and lamented about how I could have prevented it. Again, I got help.

Some other symptoms of depression include loss of appetite, loss of interest in normal activities, feeling worthless or guilty, and thoughts of death or suicide. Know that help is available. It's possible to feel sad but not have clinical depression; however, if one is suffering a traumatic loss (death of a loved one, physical assault, job loss, or separation, etc.) it may be depression, and a medical diagnosis is appropriate.

My Treatment

Since founding the Jon Francis Foundation in 2007, we have worked with more than forty-five families in missing-person situations in nineteen states and in Canada—reaching out, validating their loss, providing grief counseling and advice, and conducting searches for missing-persons. I have seen for myself that those with a missing loved one will often behave similarly to victims of sexual assault or childhood abuse.

To deal with my own brain trauma and primitive thinking, which included clinical depression, I chose medical intervention and talk therapy on both occasions.

The combination restored my brain chemistry and my ability to think and act rationally (although not everyone agrees with the last part). Taking an antidepressant brought healing to my brain—better living through chemistry!

I have come to know that depression is not a death sentence. Moreover, it should not be a source of shame. Depression is common, treatable, and curable. If you or someone you know is a victim of traumatic loss, seek medical intervention and professional counseling.

"Some people are sad sometimes. Some people are glad sometimes."
—Mr. Rogers

Despair

Holding ~by Jon Francis

The air is waiting,

winter is coming.

The ground exposed, barren,

ice covers and retreats.

We are made to be

patient, holding.

In Minnesota on election night in November 2006, we organized a "victory" party that was well attended by hopeful friends and supporters. I took an early lead in the returns but slipped behind as the more conservative northern precincts began reporting.

By 10:00 p.m., it was clear I lost my race. I made a brief announcement and thanked my supporters. I slept fitfully that night, lonely for Jon and questioning why I put myself and my family through the stress and pain of a political campaign.

Just before Christmas 2006, our five-year-old grandson, Stevie, asked me if I had won or lost the election. I said, "Well, Stevie, I lost."

He surprised and delighted me by asking, "Grandpa, how do you feel about that?"

I told him it hurt, that winning is more fun. "But Stevie, now I can spend more time with you." And he responded, "That's good."

Our summer and fall search efforts had been impressive by any standards. The hunt for Jon had now attracted national attention from the search and rescue community. But winter drove us off the mountain, and we had failed to find Jon. His body remained somewhere on the Grand Mogul, unprotected from the brutal weather and hungry predators. No parent, family, or human being should *ever* have to endure such imaginings.

We would not be able return to the mountain until mid-June at the earliest in light of the severe, unpredictable Idaho mountain climate. Linda and I held onto each other tightly for months as we weathered emotional storms, days of despair, and evenings of tears.

Jon's loss changed everything. My life was now divided between the promising time before the day Jon disappeared and the hopeless time afterward.

We had changed Jon's address from Utah to ours in Minnesota. Every letter that came addressed to Jonathan Francis tore at my heart. His letter of acceptance to Luther Theological Seminary in St. Paul was another stabbing reminder of Jon's promise, his life of ministry and service that would never be fulfilled.

With no standing and no death certificate to resolve his estate, multiple collection letters and phone calls ground on unabated. The phone conversation was almost always the same:

"Is Jonathan Francis there?"

"No. This is his father. Can I help you?"

"No, this is a personal matter for Jonathan."

"I'm sorry. My son died in a mountain climbing accident in July."

"I see. Goodbye."

We began to face all the special days without Jon, our first Thanksgiving without Jon, our first Christmas without Jon. We still carried out many of the family Christmas rituals, but holiday joy had become holiday sorrow. We decided to sell Jon's car because it was too emotionally difficult to keep. Since we couldn't own or legally sell it, we stopped payments, and it was predictably repossessed after a painful three-month collection process.

When I was finally able to look at the contents of Jon's laptop, I found a treasure chest of Jon's writing: papers for school, letters, poems, and deep thoughts and reflections that also revealed his spiritual life. He questioned and struggled, but gave his life to God, celebrated God's creation, and committed himself to serve others with love and joy.

With this evidence of Jon's sincere dedication to helping others, I took the initial steps to start a nonprofit foundation in honor of Jon, to make a positive difference in people's lives, as Jon had, and pass on his legacy of love and service.

Linda and I wanted be more involved, informed, and helpful in the coming spring search so we took training with National Association for Search and Rescue, Inc. In our classes, we learned more about how the conduct of the official search for Jon had been mishandled by not centering the search on his last known position (LKP).

Linda and I passed our tests in time for outdoor navigation training. After we completed SAR (search and rescue) training, I began indoor wall climbing.

The entire Francis family worked together for the rest of the winter on establishing the Jon Francis Foundation (JFF) to "honor Jon's life and to mold our sorrow into hope and purpose" and to provide hope, knowledge, and resources to others who suffered the misfortune of losing a loved one in the wilderness, especially those abandoned by law enforcement.

Our parallel intention was to raise public awareness and address deficiencies in SAR capabilities, preparedness, and the lack of equitable funding—an approach similar to that of the Jacob Wetterling Foundation, which worked diligently to create the Amber Alert System; and John Walsh, father of Adam Walsh, who labored long and hard to convince the US Department of Justice to create the National Center for Missing and Exploited Children.

According to an FBI audit report in 2006, the year Jon went missing, there were eight hundred unsolved "missing persons" cases in Minnesota, and two hundred unsolved "unidentified remains" cases. A flawed official search and rescue process causes deep pain and suffering to the loved ones of those missing people.

When law enforcement stops their search without finding the lost person, the family is plunged into deep despair—with feelings of abandonment, helplessness, and hopelessness. As Linda had learned during the first year, survivors are victims of unresolved loss. Not knowing what happened, and not being able to lay your loved one to rest piles grief upon grief.

In keeping with the old proverb, "Rather than curse the darkness," the Francis family decided to light a candle. We would "walk in the light" and face the world as Jon's representatives.

"UPON A FOUNDATION, HOPE"

By Mark Brouwer, *Stillwater Courier*

Wednesday, April 18, 2007

When David Francis lost his son Jon to an Idaho mountain last July, he didn't know much about search and rescue operations. Now he knows more than he could ever have wanted.

Over three dizzying days, the father of four learned that Jon had gone missing during a climb near the church camp where he worked, had rushed with his family to join an official search, and then watched as that search was called off by authorities just as it seemed to be finding its feet.

In the weeks and months that followed, the Francis family exhausted its bodies and their finances in repeated, private searches of the mountain, which gave them clues but no resolution to their ordeal. Rather than let their bitterly earned expertise go to waste, however, the family has started a foundation so that others who lose loved ones in the wilderness have more resources, direction and hope at their ready.

The family began work on The Jon Francis Foundation after a conversation David Francis had this winter with Nancy Sabin, executive director of the Jacob Wetterling Foundation, which had assisted the Francis family by providing a lost person expert last summer. That foundation (created in the aftermath of the 1989 disappearance of St. Joseph boy Jacob Wetterling) was instrumental in the search. Sabin suggested that the Francis family "consider finding a way to bring some good out of their loss."

Takeaways

Understand and recognize that depression (major depressive disorder) is a common and serious medical illness that negatively affects how you feel, think, and act. And fortunately, it's treatable.

Many grief travelers were originally ambushed by a traumatic loss or terrifying event that triggered depression, acute stress disorder, or posttraumatic stress disorder. Be alert for signs of confusion, anger, anxiety, inability to control emotions, fear, sadness, and/or shame, and do not be afraid to seek help. Remember that depression is curable.

Thomas Attig, a philosopher who wrote *How We Grieve,* reminds us that when we love others, we can easily care about what they cared about and share their concerns and values. Our loved one's causes can give meaning to our lives as survivors. We can walk in the world as their representatives.

CHAPTER 5

ON THE SUMMIT

"When he has found it, he lays it on his shoulders and rejoices. And when he comes home, he calls together his friends and his neighbors, saying to them 'Rejoice with me, for I have found my sheep that was lost.'"—Luke 15: 5–6

As spring 2007 approached, I was haunted by a vision that our son's once-handsome face and strong body were now skeletal remains. I desperately wanted to find Jon before there was nothing left. But I didn't want to be the one to find him.

We held the Jon Francis Foundation kickoff at Ascension Lutheran in Ogden, Utah, on March 5 (the day that would have been Jon's twenty-fifth birthday). We gratefully embraced the Mighty Ascension Search Team and many people in Utah who knew and loved Jon. I spoke at the well-attended banquet and participated in the evening festivities and memorials. Though the event was a blur to me, Linda and I agreed on the way home that we were glad to be immersed in one of Jon's most loving communities of faith.

A number of track events and races held that spring honored Jon in various ways. He was recognized in our hometown newspaper, the *Stillwater Gazette*. His coach paid tribute to Jon by saying, "One of the things with naming an athletic event after somebody is that you don't dwell on the sorrow or the mournful part of it; you rejoice."

Jon's Ascension West faith community in Ogden invited me to run in their annual 5K Grace Race that they dedicated to Jon in May. The race shirt had Jon's picture on it.

I flew there on my own and visited the Ogden Botanical Garden to see the tree planted by Jon's friends from the Huntsville Public Library where he had worked part-time. The previous fall, their grieving staff had planted the Burr oak (Jonathan) tree. I had sat for an hour near it, weeping and speaking to my son, saying, "Jon, I miss you."

Dad, I'm fine . . . Dad, you've never been a sad person; don't be sad now.

"Easy for you to say, Jon . . . Jon, I love you."

I love you, Dad

While sitting near the tree, I thought about one of Jon's favorite Bible verses—one that inspired him as a runner and as a youth minister: "He gives power to the faint, and strengthens the powerless. Even youths will faint and be weary, and the young will fall exhausted; but those who wait for the LORD shall renew their strength, they shall mount up with wings like eagles, they shall run and not be weary, they shall walk and not faint." (Isaiah 40: 29–31)

At home, Linda completed work on her Jon Francis Foundation JFF Safety Kit with wilderness safety and survival tips, a loud whistle, and a mirror. Such low-cost, low-tech signaling devices can be invaluable to a person lost in the wild. We held one last JFF informational meeting and fundraiser before Linda and I headed back to Idaho.

We created a presentation that documented the long, complex search for Jon. Members of our church, Ascension Episcopal, JFF directors, and members of our community were shocked at the rugged, treacherous terrain we were covering on the massive mountain.

Preparing for our return to Idaho, we rented a house in Sawtooth City in June and planned to stay in Idaho until we found Jon. I sent a letter to the Custer County sheriff to inform him that we were returning to Idaho in June, and that we would request his help in carrying Jon's remains off the mountain.

Still holding bitter memories of our months in communications hell the year before, we set up our new command center with house phones, cellphones, computers, and internet service. A well-worn, seventeen-foot fiberglass Bayliner with a 115 HP Mercury outboard, (which we purchased in Boise) arrived. We named it "Searching for Jon."

The boat reduced the expense of shuttle fees across Redfish Lake. We had aerial photos, maps, and an Incident Action Plan (IAP)—a plan to guide the spring search.

The assembled team was ready to go on the morning of June 15. I carried a fifty-pound backpack with my camping equipment, safety gear, first-aid kit, food, and water. We climbed to a small lake at 8,500 feet. We made camp that night with the help of the Sawtooth Mountain Guides who provided tents, food, and water purification. Canine teams from three states were at our base camp. Ground teams were comprised of skilled mountaineers from around the US. Resting the people and dogs at a high camp gave us more time and energy to search high on the summit block. That's where Jon was—somewhere on the summit block, on the rock above the tree line.

The next morning we began the climb to the 9,733-foot summit of the Grand Mogul. I wanted to honor Jon at the top and try to get into his head to figure out which descent route might have looked the most attractive to him.

After several hours of slogging through a thirty-to-forty degree slope of loose scree, we arrived on the summit block and made our way around giant boulders. At three-hundred feet before the summit, we donned safety helmets and roped up. As I was pulled around a large boulder with no foothold, I felt the danger. If anything had gone wrong, I would have fallen hundreds of feet to my death. Four of us worked as a team scrambling, pulling, and being pulled up until we finally stood at the summit. The view was spectacular and breathtaking.

I opened the rusty ammunition box that held the summit log of handwritten entries going back to 1965. I added mine:

"David Francis, June 16, 2007. Stillwater, Minnesota. Father of Jon Francis. Climbed from the tarn to search for and honor my son Jon, missing since July 15, 2006."

I wondered again, *God, where were you? Why didn't you guide Jon's feet off this mountain?*

For fifteen days, we joined with dog teams and ground teams to search the mountain, forest, and surrounding lake. But by June 30, we had totaled more than fifty search days without success. I felt waves of hopelessness. I feared we'd never find Jon's body.

We issued a press release asking for more volunteers and we asked experts for advice. Their analysis of our results suggested a new plan. We would focus our attention where the majority of accidents and rescues on the Grand Mogul took place—the north face where there were several huge crevasses. Going into the most treacherous terrain on the Grand Mogul was our best hope of finding Jon. Twenty-five years after holding my newborn son, feeling joy and hope for his future, my remaining hope was that we could find his body and lay him to rest with dignity.

At my request, the exhausted but committed mountain guides roped up and climbed, rappelled, and searched several gullies on the north side for two days before a summer intern spotted a bright object in a snow pack at the end of a long day. The object was a buckle from Jon's backpack. Jon's remains were nearby.

When I received the call that Jon had been found, I felt a brief elation before grief poured in. Never again could there be the slightest hope that our son was alive. We now had the physical proof—the remains were the evidence. Our son was dead.

Due to the late hour, the crime scene investigation and the transport of Jon's remains off the mountain had to wait until morning. The guides marked the location with a cairn, set up camp, and held a vigil. I decided not to climb to the place where they found Jon. I accepted the gift given to me by others to keep my final memory of him to be his handsome smile and warm embrace —not his skeletal remains scattered on the rocks.

Linda had been carrying Jon's dental records for months, and they were used to make a positive identification. We focused on the safe-keeping of Jon's remains so we could bring Jon home for burial.

Now that the long search was finally over, Linda and I were again filled with questions. Why did Jon decide to climb the Grand Mogul alone? Why did he choose to descend the north face? What happened? Why did he fall? What decisions and steps led to his death on the mountain? We wanted to know, but at the same time, we didn't want to know.

The coroner ruled the cause of Jon's death as "massive, blunt force trauma to his head." From all appearances, Jon had a long fall and his death was immediate. That answered one of the important questions that had haunted us: Did Jon suffer? We felt some solace to know that he died instantly.

We had learned that most climbing accidents are caused by human error and unfortunate decisions, and most accidents occur on the descent when climbers are tired and may be in a hurry to get back down. The north face appeared to be the most direct route from the summit. Was Jon was in a hurry to catch the 3:00 p.m. shuttle? Did he even know how challenging a north face descent would be? If so, maybe he chose the challenge, trusting in his strength and climbing experience.

I don't know how Jon felt at the time. We know only that he lost his footing and slipped, or tripped, and fell.

Jon usually climbed with partners who told us he was cautious by nature—not reckless. He had tried to find a partner for his climb of the

Grand Mogul on that Saturday but when none were available, he decided to climb solo. Would it have made a difference if Jon had not been alone? There are many questions we can never answer.

Takeaways

Unresolved loss, not knowing where your loved one is, or what happened, piles grief upon grief.

Unresolved loss is distressful and can lead to mental and physical illnesses and emotional upheaval.

CHAPTER 6

MOURNING: HOW DO I GO ON LIVING?

As black clouds hovered over the Grand Mogul, I directed my thoughts toward the mountain: *Jon, I love you. Jon, I miss you. I lift you up and place you in the arms of God.*

For reasons I still do not understand, I accepted the reality of Jon's death that day and began to mourn the loss of my son.

In *Grief Counseling and Grief Therapy,* J. William Worden describes four "tasks" of mourning. The first is to accept the loss. I had just faced the reality that Jon was not coming back. The second task is to process the pain of grief. I would have to travel a long and lonely road to work through the enormous pain I felt that day.

Worden's third task is to adjust to life without the person who is gone. This task involves adjustments in every part of life including changes in my sense of self: Who is this father without a son? How have I changed with this loss? How do I see the world now with this vast emptiness? This extends to our spiritual selves as well. I was angry with God for allowing this to happen to my son, and to me. I would have to find a new meaning—to find a way for this loss to make sense and gain a sense of control over my life.

I was absolutely experiencing the "intense regression" that Worden suggests that bereavement can lead to. I felt helpless in the face of this loss. I felt inadequate; I had been unable to prevent what had happened to Jon. Though I did not yet know how to adjust to life without my son, Worden assures us that it is possible for the negative images to fade over time in favor of more positive ones.

Worden's final task is to find ways to remember our loved ones in ways that don't prevent us from living our everyday lives. This is where a grief counselor can be helpful. We are still able to find joy in loving others as well as still loving our lost loved one.

Worden calls the grief of losing a child "complicated." I found this to be a sad truth. I would continue to feel grief in the form of longing for my son, loneliness, negative thoughts, as well as anger and bitterness at the circumstances of Jon's death. However, I could not live in denial. The facts were there. My emotional reactions to frequent memories are still fresh even after long periods of relative peace. Working through Worden's four tasks would be an ongoing challenge.

Cries of Grief

I turned again to my friend Father Jerry with my questioning. Jerry recalled the words of Pascal, "God did not come into the world to take away suffering; God came to lend his presence to it."

He assured me that God was present when Jon fell to his death. God was present in the volunteers who came to help. God is present in all the money that was raised to help others in similar circumstances.

God is present in all the grief and prayers for Jon.

Even as time has passed, I continue to wonder why God didn't guide Jon's steps safely off the mountain. Jon served and glorified God with his words and deeds, his running and his climbing. The Psalmist promises that angels watch over us: "For he shall give his angels charge over you, to keep you in all your ways. On their hands they will bear you up, lest you dash your foot against a stone."

Losing my son jarred me from a place of assurance in my beliefs to a place of questioning. Having no resolution, I decided to follow in my son's footsteps—I will walk the questioning, listening, praying, and receiving paths. I will strive to accept and love, as Jon did, "imperfect people, an imperfect world, and an imperfect God."

"Time does not heal. Prayer heals. The Holy Spirit Heals. You choose to heal . . ." I found that quote in *Five Cries of Grief: One Family's Journey to Healing after the Tragic Death of a Son* by Merton and A. Irene Strommen—a powerful story that describes their journey through grief to healing after losing their son, Dave.

David (Dave) Strommen, age twenty-five, from Minnesota, was serving as a youth minister at Frontier Ranch, a Young Life Camp on a slope of Mount Princeton in Colorado. On August 12, 1986, he was struck and killed instantly by a bolt of lightning. I found the similarity between Dave's story and Jon's eerie and poignant: Jonathan (Jon) Francis, age twenty-four, was serving as a youth minister at Luther Heights Camp in Sawtooth Mountains of Idaho. On July 15, 2006, Jon fell on a mountain and died instantly.

The Strommens each write about their son, and his death, from the perspective of a father and of a mother as they experience what they call their Five Cries of Grief. In the first, "the cry of pain," they talk about their indescribable personal pain.

The mother feels as though some-thing has been "wrenched, ripped, and torn" from her—in a storm of pain that she would not avoid, but "lean into" and "go through."

The father describes being literally "bent low in grief." He shared the feeling of a loved one being "torn" from his body and the personal loss of a significant part of his own future.

The second cry, "a cry of longing," refers to their ever-present loneliness and the longing for some sense of their son's physical presence—the familiar associations, his belongings, special occasions, objects and locations, his friends, and the multitude of meaningful memories of being together.

Linda and I were awash in these longings. One of the hardest longings for me is associated with Jon's clothing and running shoes.

It's been more than thirteen years, and I am still unable to give anything away. They are stored in his closet and in many boxes. I especially cling to Jon's running shoes.

Jon's shoes
So many shoes.
White Adidas,
Blue Nike,
Worn cleats,

Asics—

His favorite.

Reminders of his gift.

Reminders of his passion.

Reminders of our loss.

—David Francis

The Strommens' third cry, "the cry for supportive love," is a cry that has been answered for Linda and me in many ways. We are grateful for the support of our family, the many people around us who helped mightily in the search for Jon, who gave us hugs and words of love and support in letters and in person. Just as Irene described needing to be around Dave's friends, Linda and I wanted to be around Jon's friends, work associates, kids he mentored, and those who shared stories with us about Jon. Our community of faith supported us and consoled us.

The fourth cry, "the cry for understanding," has been a tough one for me. Though I was finally able to accept what had happened to Jon, I struggled to understand why it happened. What good could I find in this seemingly senseless tragedy? I shared Merten's questions of God. Why draw our son to a ministry in the first place then cut short his life? What is the divine plan in this? I still struggle with this, but I have endeavored to lean on my own faith. "I lift up my eyes to the hills— from where will my help come? My help comes from the LORD, who made heaven and earth. —Psalm 121:1–2

Grief experts know that the death of a loved one often creates a faith crisis in those who believe in a loving God. Each individual needs to find a way to understand and accept "divine mysteries." But how can such a God permit the unfathomable pain of losing a child? Humans must find ways to make sense of the chaos of the world.

Many have asked me if I am angry with God. My reply has not changed, "No I am not angry with God. I'm just highly disappointed." Again and again I still wonder, *God where were you on July 15, 2006? Why didn't you guide, your servant, Jon's feet off that mountain?*

The Strommens chose to lean mightily on their faith. Rather than continue to ask why and to search for answers, they accepted that God mourns with them and wants them to heal, learn, and grow from their heart-wrenching experience. This also helped with their fifth and final cry— the "cry for significance." They chose to "transform their grief into growth." They focused on serving others, their family and their church, and on appreciating the everyday aspects of life.

Irene found journaling and writing a book with Merten about their loss another way to serve others who've suffered similar circumstances. They organized a road race in their son's memory and continue to extend Dave's Youth Ministry of friendship and caring for others. To that end, Merton established an endowed fund and a Youth and Family Institute at Augsburg College in Minneapolis to train others to serve in a youth and family ministry.

Jon was four years old when Dave Strommen died. While raising Jon and enjoying his unconditional love, I had no knowledge of the Strommens' journey through the valley of grief. While reading *Five*

Cries of Grief, I was dumbstruck by so many of the similarities between our sons, our common experiences, and our intense motivation to honor our sons' memories and salvage some good from our shared loss.

For many years, we held a Jon Francis Half-Marathon, similar to the Dave Strommen Road Race. We created the Jon Francis Foundation, similar to the Youth and Family Institute at Augsburg.

We created JFF Wilderness Safety Education and Scholarships, similar to the Strommen Endowed chair at Augsburg. JFF organized a wilderness safety camp named Camp Jon. And we have each written books about our losses and our grief.

Bringing Jon Home

In August 2007 I boarded the plane to transport Jon's remains back to Minnesota. Linda stayed in Idaho. From the window of the plane, I watched the baggage conveyor to try to catch sight of any of the "special care" that I was told the handlers would use with the package labeled, "HUMAN REMAINS." I couldn't see anything. During the flight, I read *Lament for a Son* again. This third time, I was able to read it without tears streaming down my face.

At the VIP baggage area in the Twin Cities International Airport terminal, I finally saw the package containing Jon's remains. I was stunned and horrified when I saw how small the package was. This is all that was left of my son—fragments and bones in a cardboard box!

Our daughter Melissa met me at the funeral home. Her face revealed the same horror at seeing what was left of her brother. Her beautiful face turned into a mask of agony. "Dad, he's in a box!" She too felt the cruel reality of what had happened to her only brother.

The next day, I would head back to Idaho to continue the search for more of Jon's remains. I did not want to leave any part of my son on that mountain.

Before leaving I spoke with Father Jerry and the funeral home representative to arrange Jon's funeral and burial. Linda and I had agreed that Jon would approve of cremation as an environmentally responsible choice.

I visited Rutherford Hill Cemetery, only a short walk from our house. Established in 1851, Rutherford Hill harbors the gravestone markers of old pioneer families including children even younger than Jon. I was drawn to the lone columbarium standing behind cemetery hill on flat ground, surrounded by green space, and facing a wall constructed of boulders. The horizon was abundant with trees. This place felt like an island sanctuary in a sea of noise, traffic, commerce, and unceasing human activity—a fitting place to lay Jon to rest.

Back in Idaho, members of the Sawtooth Mountain Guides had ascended the crack system above the gulley where Jon's remains had been recovered and found his backpack and some more bone fragments. They found his clothes, car keys, the ten essentials, and his camera in the pack. When we downloaded the memory chip into our computer, Jon's gifts to us were the pictures he took while standing on the summit. I was able to imagine the same now-familiar scene through my son's eyes. (Jon's summit photo is the beautiful book cover.)

Unfortunately the Custer County Sheriff's Office would not organize any other recovery efforts. The Sawtooth Mountain Guides went up one more time and found no more bones or fragments. Jon's remains had been found in a snow pack that had slowly melted away.

I made my last climb into the north face. The place where I stood was not a romantic, snow-covered, alpine mountain. This was no Shangri-La. I still become angry when anyone suggests that my son died in a beautiful, natural place where he loved to be. I spent a day with a small group that dug through other snow packs in hope that we might find more scattered fragments. We found none.

By late August, with no results after several more teams searched, we took the *Searching for Jon* boat out of the water. We stopped our efforts. We would not risk the safety of others with further searches.

At a thank you and farewell dinner gathering at Redfish Lake Lodge, we expressed our deep appreciation to the group who risked their own safety to help us find Jon. Not since my days as a submarine officer had I felt such depth of admiration and gratitude toward a crew of people.

We made one more trip across Redfish Lake that summer. On the north side of the Grand Mogul, a small, unnamed lake had become a landmark and rendezvous point during our searches. On our first summer there, we began to refer to the tranquil water as "Lake Jon."

Linda had commissioned Wayne at the Smiley Creek Café to construct a sign to place on the shore of Lake Jon. Linda, Jocelyn, Doug, and I, along with the kids, hiked to Lake Jon and ate lunch on the shore before securing the sign in the ground.

I thought of the 23rd Psalm, "The Lord is my shepherd, I shall not want. He makes me lie down in green pastures; He leads me beside still waters; he restores my soul . . ."

We don't know how long the Lake Jon marker will stay there. But our broken hearts will remain there forever.

Takeaways

Consider Worden's four tasks of grieving: accept the loss, process the pain of grief, adjust without the deceased, and live effectively in the world despite our loss.

Consider Strommens' Five Cries of Grief: the cry of pain, the cry of longing, the cry for supportive love, the cry for understanding, and the cry for significance.

Gatherings and events with friends, neighbors, faith communities, support groups, and even with strangers can be helpful activities to remember and to honor your loved one.

Gaining some level of resolution is helped by providing any kind of service to others, joining a group that performs outreach to help others, or adopting a cause.

Find ways to honor the life of your loved one.

Hold events of remembering: funerals, rituals, memorials.

Closure is a myth. However, through our grief work, we can achieve some degree of resolution to our loss.

CHAPTER 7

SURVIVING, HEALING, RESOLVING

In the early years of our loss, Linda and I met with a couple who had lost a child eight years earlier. They shared with us that they began to feel "normal" about seven years after the death. I refused to believe them. In my mind, I believed that I would never again feel "normal."

However, I did. Around 2012, six years after Jon's death, joy and even laughter began creeping into my life again. Sometimes I fought it. But it happened anyway. However, I had to survive many years and do a lot of grief work before I arrived at the "normal" years.

Many grief books have been helpful to me. One of the most valuable to me on my journey is *How To Go On Living When Someone You Love Dies*, by Therese Rando, PhD. Dr. Rando places quotation marks around the word "resolving" when she discusses grief. She asserts that grief over a "truly significant" loss can never be entirely resolved or "settled" permanently. Resolution of any kind can only come through continuing with our "grief work."

In my eulogy to my son Jon, I said, "There is no closure. Closure is for bank accounts, not love accounts." The best we can hope for and work toward is some resolution to our grief. But resolution will only come with time and our continued grief work.

As Rando says, "We cannot wave a magic wand and make it all go away." Dr. Rando recommends that we follow a process that begins with acknowledging and understanding the loss. Our need to understand and feel a sense of control over something that has completely upended our lives is why we often can't help thinking about what happened to our loved one—even reconstruct the circumstances to figure out what we might have done to prevent the tragic outcome.

Letting ourselves feel the pain instead of avoiding it or pushing it away—as tempting as that is. Letting it out is a way to let it go. "Yield to it to in order to move through it."

If we allow ourselves to experience all of the feelings, we will embark on the journey through grief that will follow the necessary steps that will lead us to some healing and a form of resolution. The key point is to make the decision to work through the process and give yourself permission to feel whatever you feel along the way. We can find ways to adapt our lives to new thinking, new activities, new energy, and new love.

To allow joy back into our lives is not a betrayal of the person we have lost. Love is not a fixed commodity, there is always more to go around. Figuring out what we need and asking for help from others will help us move forward. Reading and learning more about grief and loss in books were invaluable in helping me to understand that life can feel good again.

Rando echoes the Strommens and others who endorse seeking

support from our faith, our faith communities, and grief groups. We deserve to and can feel better. If medical intervention is needed, we must not be deterred by any preconceived notions or views that we should be able to handle whatever life throws at us without help.

The best way to help others grieve is to grieve well ourselves. We are better role models for our loved ones if we take care of ourselves. We don't need to be thinking about our grief and pain all the time—we can also focus on the living and reconnect with others.

Part of the process that Rando describes is a tall mountain for me to climb—the idea of letting go—"separation"—from the need to have our loved one with us in this world. I was so consumed with anger, sadness, emptiness, and loneliness that I only felt the hole in my heart where Jon once lived. Like the Strommens, I felt as though a part of my body had been ripped away. I had lost a piece of my soul.

In tragic circumstances where we cannot find our missing loved one's body (such as a wilderness loss or "missing in action" in a war) survivors may suffer from "ambiguous" loss and complicated grief.

Dr. Pauline Boss, author of *Ambiguous Loss: Learning to Live with Unresolved Grief,* studied the impact of this type of loss on survivors. The distress involved can lead to a range of difficulties: "depressive episodes, physical illness, emotional upheaval, and family conflict." This can be especially true in the case of a sudden or accidental death.

This is why I spent seventy days searching on the Grand Mogul and returned many times to the "scene of the accident." I was desperately driven to find my son's body, understand what led to his death, and lay him to rest. Since we began working with families through the Jon Francis Foundation, most of the people we have engaged with described feeling the same emotion—the agony of unresolved loss.

We mourn for the lost presence of our loved one, our lost future with our loved one, and the loss of our spoken and unspoken dreams and expectations. I will never experience the joys I had hoped for with my son: his ordination, his marriage, his becoming a father, all the future birthdays and holidays, and camping again with him under a canopy of stars.

Letters and Journals

Most grief therapists and grief travelers recommend that we put our pain on paper. Writing about our lost love is highly therapeutic and beneficial. I encourage you, if you have not already, to sit down and quietly write about your pain.

Our daughter Jocelyn and our son Jon, although born fourteen years apart, grew to be soul mates. If anyone on this planet is sadder than I am over Jon's death, it is Jocelyn.

She wrote:

"A big part of me died on July 15th, 2006. Jon was my baby brother, but I looked up to him and I think in some ways we completed each other—I was put on earth to loosen him up and he was put on earth to mellow me out. There was mutual respect, admiration, and love between us—he frequently amazed me with his wise-beyond-his-years perspective and thoughtfulness.

Jon and I shared a love of many things—music, food (okay, candy), sports, hiking, camping, the Spanish language and culture, traveling, thrift shopping, and just plain having fun. I find myself listening to our mutually adored bands on a daily basis, and I doubt I will ever be able to make it through "Landslide" by Stevie Nicks without crying. It was first recorded by Fleetwood Mac and then the Dixie Chicks (yes, Jon and I both LOVE the Dixie Chicks). I miss him, but listening to the music we love fills me with his spirit and energy."

Go Forth, Jon

Before Jon's cremation and funeral, Linda and I agreed to the examination of Jon's remains by a forensic anthropologist in St. Paul. I would not read the report, but I wanted confirmation of what we had learned already about the cause of Jon's death, and whether he may have lingered and/or suffered. The results confirmed that Jon died of "blunt force trauma" to his head. He had fallen a very long way. We learned that re-growth of bone takes place quickly as an injured body tries to heal itself. There was no evidence of bone re-growth; Jon's death was immediate.

When Linda and I visited the funeral home to select an urn, I felt close to a panic attack. We chose a Minnesota cherry wood box and inscribed on it selected words from the Celtic Funeral Service:

"Go forth Jon, son, brother, friend, servant of God, Christian soul." We chose a niche facing west at Rutherford Cemetery.

When a friend suggested that we scatter some of Jon's ashes on the

Grand Mogul, Linda was firm, "No, there's enough of Jon on that mountain."

The Funeral

The Francis family gathered at Ascension Church on October 9, 2007, to honor our son's spirit for a second time and grieve for his lost life. The church was full of Jon's friends, loved ones, and one searcher who had been with us from the very beginning, Jim Hanley, with his dog Shania. I sat with Linda and our daughters in the front pew.

The music, Bible verses, and prayers of the Celtic funeral service were interspersed with some of Jon's favorite poems read by his sisters and friends.

I stood to read Jon's words, "Make connections; let rip with joy . . . My bursting forth takes the form of celebration, of grace, of awe and wonder, of humility and of thanksgiving. I am celebrating the goodness of nature. I am thankful for the goodness of the created world. I do not know why, but I am closer to God when I am outside . . . I give glory to God for her abundant creation. There is goodness all round. There is goodness deep within."

I was carried along by the beauty of the poetry and the music— drawn into a euphoric feeling—all this to honor Jon. Father Jerry's homily reminded us that Jon saw God in all creation and knew it was all good. He encouraged us to see Jon in every sunrise, in the moon coming up over the water, the leaves changing in the fall, and flowers in the spring.

Embracing my son's urn, I broke down for the first time in public. Fierce tears stung my face as I passed the mournful faces all around me. At the cemetery, mourners gathered around me at the niche. But I couldn't let go; I continued to grip the box. Father Jerry gently told me it was time to place the box in the marble vault. Finally and carefully, I placed my son's remains inside his tomb.

I sprinkled a handful of sand over the box. Sand that Linda and I had collected from the lakes Jon loved and once played near—Lake Michigan, Redfish Lake, and Little Carnelian Lake. Our fellow mourners formed a silent, solemn line and each, in turn, sprinkled sand on Jon's consecrated, final resting place.

As the slow procession moved by, I thought back to our first vigil held in view of the Grand Mogul, and my first farewell to our son, Jon, *I love you. Jon, I miss you. You are gone. You have passed over. My soul is torn. I will lift you up and place you into the arms of God.*

I led the assembly in reading his committal: "Jonathan, I bless you; I release you. I set you free; I set me free. I let you be; I let me be. Go forth Jon, son, brother, friend, servant of God, Christian soul, in the name of God who knows you and with the blessing of those who love you."

The caretaker came forward and fastened the door shut to the niche. As everyone huddled in the cold wind, Linda and I hugged as many people as we could before leaving. Then we walked away slowly to live the remainder of our lives, to learn and somehow to bear the empty hole in our hearts that is life without our son Jon.

Shortly after the funeral, The Reverend LeeAnne Watkins, Jon's youth minister, sent me a copy of the homily she wrote the day we buried Jon:

My heart hurts. I helped bury a young man today. I stood in the autumn wind and watched as his father placed the small box, which contained what was left of his son, into a vault. The boy's name was Jon Francis. He was the quietest member of my youth group out at Ascension Church in Stillwater. Jon and his family were very good to me when I took the job out there, fresh out of seminary.

Today I kept thinking of all the Thursday night youth groups, church lock-ins, and the trips to a summer cabin singing, *"Bye, Bye, Miss American Pie."*

I remembered him playing chess with his mentor at the House of Prayer retreat. I thought of what a leader he was in the Teens Encounter Christ weekends, he seemed so steady and solid and prayerful. He laughed often . . .

Today I thought of the vacation Bible school we did with homeless youth in Minneapolis, and how even though he was so small in stature, the children climbed all over him, and he was tender and gentle with them, so attentive and sensitive; and it was obvious that he had a gift in working with children.

I thought today of how he has been the only young person I've sponsored for confirmation as young as sixteen. He wanted to be confirmed, and so I made him sit down with me and explain why . . . That day he started talking about God and just couldn't stop, and one-

and-a-half-hours later, we were both in tears at how wondrous and lavish our God is. I have rarely seen such depth of faith in anyone, no matter their age. Jon's heart was as open to God as God's was to him. A beautiful thing.

And today we buried him, finally, beautifully, each of us sprinkling over him a handful of sand from one of his favorite lakes. And my heart hurts. It hurts because I'm now a parent and the thought of losing my child makes my blood turn cold. It hurts because Jon had such promise as a youth minister, a pastor, and a theologian. It hurts because, well, because I opened my heart to him and my life is changed because of him, and now he's dead.

I can fret and try to protect those I love, but I will fail. Life is fragile. Knowledge of that is terrifying.

There's a good case to be made for never opening a heart to love, because it hurts. The risk is great. An open heart is an unprotected heart. But love we do, because God is love.

And God first loved us. And God is in us. And there are times of great joy and laughter and amazement when you love with open hearts. Jon's life and his death teach that. Love is worth it.

And that's what church is. Jon was giving his life for this idea, because he understood what church is, people bound together in love by a loving God.

Today I saw those youth group members all grown up, stuffed into suits and wiping their eyes. I saw elders climbing the stairs to Eucharist. I heard children singing, *"There is wideness to God's mercy."* I saw church.

Such brave lovers. Such holiness. Jon's people, chock full of love, living with open hearts, and showing up even when, especially when, our hearts hurt, and loving still.

LeeAnne is right. An open heart is an unprotected heart, and life is fleeting and fragile. But love is hardy and enduring.

Takeaways

Funerals are not for those who have died; they are for the living.

Funerals can be an important event in our grief journey.

Funerals and Celebrations of Life provide many benefits including helping us acknowledge our loss, accepting the support of others, and honoring our loved one.

Writing about our lost love is therapeutic and beneficial.

CHAPTER 8

REMEMBERING: NEVER FORGET ME

"If there ever comes a time when we can't be together,
keep me in your heart, I'll stay there forever."

—Winnie the Pooh

My grief work has taken many paths. I delayed. I ignored. I avoided. Then I faced my grief head on. One of my paths was to be intentional in remembering and honoring (not worshiping) Jon's life. I discovered that this was redirecting my mourning into positive action.

Although we are not Jewish, I carry an Old Testament name and we chose an Old Testament name for our son. I learned recently that when you name a Jewish child, there's a line in the ceremony: "May this be a name honored in the house of Israel."

I passionately yearn that Jon's name will be honored in every house and in every heart that knew him. An old proverb says, "When you stop mentioning your loved one's name, they die twice."

Since I was outraged when the public sector abandoned our son, I was driven to action. The Jon Francis Foundation, created originally to raise money for our yearlong search, embraced a mission to help other

families who were betrayed by the public sector. I resolved that JFF
would honor Jon's memory and bring some good from his loss by acting as a victims' advocate in missing adult children tragedies.

I had never used the word "betrayed" until we met the Swansons of
Marshall, Minnesota. Jim Hanley, our friend and search-dog handler,
called me on Memorial Day 2008 on behalf of the Swanson family. Jim
and his dog Shania were searching for Brandon Swanson, a nineteen-
year-old college student who went missing in southwestern Minnesota.

Brandon's mother, Annette, gave me some details. In the early
morning of May 14, their son Brandon had driven his car into a ditch
by a cornfield. He left his stuck car to walk to the nearest town. He was
walking and talking on his cellphone to his father, Brian, when
Brandon shouted, and his phone went dead.

When Annette called the sheriff's office to report her son's disappearance, the dispatcher said, "Well, ma'am, your son is nineteen years
old and has a right to go missing."

Law Enforcement was not required under Minnesota Law to take
any action. Annette felt betrayed.

I immediately joined other volunteers and search leaders from the
Jon Francis Foundation to begin searching for Brandon. Angered by
the early resistance and lame response from law enforcement, Annette
initiated a discussion with her representative in the Minnesota House
of Representatives regarding Minnesota missing persons' laws.

The Francis family joined the Swansons in an effort to raise the
awareness of elected officials to the lack of legal protection for missing

adult children. Together we successfully lobbied the Minnesota Legislature to pass a law extending legal protection to missing adults. The new law, named Brandon's Law, passed on July 1, 2009.

The Swanson family found a significant way to honor and to make a difference in their son Brandon's memory.

In the years since I lost my son, people have asked me how I'm doing. I distilled my responses into short sentences:

"I'm okay. But I miss Jon."

"I'm learning to live with a hole in my heart."

"The Jon Francis Foundation gives me a sense of purpose."

My calendar is populated with sad anniversaries: March 5, Jon's birthday and the last time he was with us at home; July 15, the day he died on the Grand Mogul; July 24, the day most of his remains were found; August 1, the day I brought Jon's remains home (and Linda's birthday); September 9, Jon's memorial service at Ascension Church; and October 9, 2007, the date we laid Jon to rest.

The day after Jon's funeral, I began to write. I wanted to put my pain on paper as an act of grieving and healing. I was increasingly inspired by my son's brief life. As I wrote, I often cried. I desperately wanted others to know that an uncommon young man named Jon Francis once lived and loved among us. I completed *Bringing Jon Home: The Wilderness Search for Jon Francis.* Yet I was compelled to do more. I did not want the world to forget Jon Francis, who once lived joyfully and loved boldly.

Jon loved to dance. He also understood the "divine" dance. Early in his life he caught and felt a deep faith in a creator god. He "danced" with God and became a steward of God's mysteries and His creation. Jon was a hearer of the Word and a doer, a questioner, and a seeker.

Linda and I would establish a scholarship in his name at his high school, organize Jon Francis Foundation Road Races, hold an annual wilderness safety camp named Camp Jon, and plant trees, one each year.

When I Am Among Jon's Trees

(adapted from Mary Oliver)

When I am among Jon's trees,
especially . . . the pines.
They give off such hints of gladness.
I would almost say that they save me, and daily.
I am so distant from the hope of myself . . .
Around me the trees stir in their branches
and call out, "Stay awhile."
One planted each year, since.
Twelve now, placed in the ground with love.
They call out, "Stay awhile" and remember me.

The light flows from their branches.
And they call again, "It's simple,"
they say, "and you, too, have come
into the world to do this, to go easy,
to be filled with light, and to shine."

Our remembrances will take many different forms. Yet they serve the same purpose: "Do not forget me."

Philosopher Thomas Attig stresses in his book, *How We Grieve,* that by sharing the values and concerns of our lost loved ones, we "find meaning and direction to our lives as survivors."

Jon loved and respected the wilderness, "God's wonderful creation." We in a sense walk in the world as his representative with our Wilderness Education Mission.

Attig also talks about the importance of having a realistic image of our lost loved one including their positive and their negative characteristics. This is required to hold onto that lost person in healthy ways.

Linda and I share some anger that Jon was taking risks in the wilderness. Often we think it was foolhardy and selfish. We wish we had known and shared our fears with him. I would have wanted to say something like, "Jon. Do you know how many people you would leave devastated if you were to die on a mountain alone?"

If we can recall and let ourselves feel all aspects of our loved one, our experiences with them, memories, attachments, etc., we can form a new relationship with that person. We can "choose which memories to keep and which to give up." We can replace the longing for the physical presence of the person with a more "abstract love."

Cards, letters, gatherings, memorials, and phone calls from Jon's friends often reminded me that Jon loved and accepted others unconditionally. He lived joyfully. He loved boldly. This evidence of his brief life has been a continuing source of inspiration for me.

My most enduring memories are the joy, love, and happiness that Jon brought into my life.

Takeaways

Talk to others who knew your loved one, hear their stories, and learn their perspectives.

Act on behalf of your loved one's concerns and values.

Engage in activities and rituals that your loved one found meaningful.

Hold onto the lost loved one in healthy ways by remembering special times, events, fun memories.

Share stories about your loved one.

CHAPTER 9

TOLERATING

"But did you enjoy the play, Mrs. Lincoln?"

Imagine if a theater critic had asked President Lincoln's wife, Mary Todd Lincoln, who had just witnessed the her husband's assassination, "But did you enjoy the play, Mrs. Lincoln?"

That would be incredible, unimaginable, insensitive, and stupid. Think again. People often say hurtful words to others in grief. We have all overheard conversations at funerals or perhaps even had thoughtless and clumsy comments made to us in our grief.

I recall many of the comments made to me over the years since Jon's death. They came from well-meaning and sincere people and friends who simply wanted to express their condolences and make a connection. I felt lost and confused and was searching for answers and comfort from others. Rather than feeling comforted, I often felt annoyed by some comments I heard.

"The good die young."

"He's in a better place."

"I know how you feel. Last year, my nephew died."

"Soon the grief won't be so bad."

"Be strong."

"He's in the arms of Jesus."

"It's good that you have other children."

"It was God's will."

"God needed another angel."

"You are so strong. I don't know how you do it."

The absence and/or silence of some specific important people in my life added to my distress; some of our once-close friends never called or acknowledged our loss. Further, after the funeral, as people went back to their lives, little mention was made of Jon. People rarely mentioned our son's name around us, perhaps for fear that it would upset us? But I desperately wanted to hear Jon's name. I wanted to hear and tell more stories about his life. This is still true.

The key to serenity may be to have low expectations about the ability of others to comfort us especially early in our grief. Many people are so uncomfortable with the subject of death, and so fearful of saying the wrong thing, that they often say nothing. Others truly want to help but don't know how to do it.

Henri Nouwen wrote in *Out of Solitude,* "When we honestly ask ourselves which person in our lives means the most to us, we often find that it is those who, instead of giving much advice, solutions, or cures, have chosen rather to share our pain and touch our wounds with a gentle and tender hand. The friend who can be silent with us in a moment of despair or confusion, who can stay with us in an hour of grief and bereavement, who can tolerate not knowing, not curing, not healing and face with us the reality of our powerlessness, that is a friend who cares."

Dr. Rando advises, "Do not let others' personal judgments about the meaning of your loss rob you of your grief or determine how you feel." She warns us to be careful about following "the advice of well-meaning others" and recognize that even when others try to help, they cannot really take away our pain. We must realize that others may feel "helpless" around us. Most people do not have the skills and wisdom to comfort others in our fresh, raw grief.

However, I have benefited from the experience and wisdom of those who are professional grief counselors, social workers, close friends, or "members of the club" (People who share and know our specific pain and loss.) I was introduced to the term, "members of the club" by another father who earlier had suffered the death of his son. "We are members of a club none of us ever wanted to join. And we pay a high cost to join."

From my own grief experience, this has become my compass when in the presence of those suffering from loss:

- ✓ Always validate the person's pain.
- ✓ Never try to fix it or minimize it.
- ✓ Avoid comparing your grief to theirs in an attempt to comfort.
- ✓ Less is more. Fewer words are better.
- ✓ Avoid delivering a sermon to a bereaved person.
- ✓ Give praise. Say words and stories that respect, remember, and honor the deceased.

✓ Feel kindness and compassion toward those in grief.

✓ Try to walk a mile in their moccasins.

✓ Know that your presence and your caring arms (not your words) bring the most comfort.

✓ Call, write, and/or visit after the funeral. (This is the loneliest time.)

✓ Send sympathy letters and cards.

✓ Make a donation in the name of the deceased to a cause s/he cared about.

✓ If you have them, tell fond, heartwarming, and even humorous stories about the deceased. Fond stories are treasures that will bring a smile, lighten our hearts, and last a lifetime. Send them in your letters.

✓ Send pictures along with your stories of happy and meaningful events.

✓ Finally, I believe this is the most comforting and caring discussion: If you can do this with sincerity, relate how important the deceased was in your life. How his/her life, principles, or practices made you a better person. Did s/he model behavior that you adopted? Did s/he give you some sage advice, guidance, or help that made a positive difference in your life's journey? These stories can affirm the value of your loved one's life. Obituaries are often filled with the person's accomplishments and offspring. The best ones describe how the deceased positively affected others.

While creating this list, it hit me that I was applying my business training. This list could be termed, "Best practices when dealing with someone in grief."

Many years ago, my wife Linda and I were sitting with one of our dearest friends, Sally. Sally's husband, Don, had just died in hospice care. I struggled to find ways to meet her grief needs.

Finally I said, "Well, Sally, if there is nothing I can do, I will go home and polish my shoes for Don's funeral."

Sally responded, "Please take my shoes with you and polish them." Sally relieved my ache and gave me a sense of purpose.

The internet has become an important vehicle to find information and knowledge and stay in contact with others. In addition, social media and electronic mail (Facebook, Twitter, Instagram, Google, etc.) have become popular and widespread. We have likely received a Facebook notification of the death of someone we know. I struggle with this. Why? For me, and for many in my generation, an email does not have the same warmth and compassion as a letter, phone call, or sympathy card. However, the internet has become a socially acceptable and common way to stay connected.

If you use the internet, be sure to use it to inform others and to express your sympathy to those in grief. Posting pictures and messages on Facebook may well bring some comfort and healing to others. If this sounds like a lukewarm endorsement for the consoling power of the internet, it is! On the other hand, I will never forget the meaningful and comforting electronic mail message I received from Alla Bozarth, priest, poet, grief counselor, and author. On July 15, 2007, the first anniversary of Jon's death, Alla wrote, "David and Linda, Today I will light a candle to celebrate Jon's birthday into paradise."

Takeaway

Consider how you can appropriately show support and comfort others in their grief.

CHAPTER 10

GRIEF TRAVELERS

"We were young. We have died. Remember us."
—"The Young Dead Soldiers Do Not Speak"
poem by Archibald MacLeish

One of the most comprehensive books I've read on surviving, coping, and healing after loss is *I Wasn't Ready to Say Goodbye* by Brook Noel and Pamela Blair. Noel and Blair cover the wideness of human suffering. I highly recommend their book, which offers a sensitive, compassionate, and timely discussion of grief and loss in military life.

As a veteran, I read this section with interest and appreciation as I was reminded of the thousands of casualties, tragic losses, trauma, sacrifices, and deaths suffered by our service members and military families. Thousands of Missing in Action (MIAs) have left behind millions of survivors suffering from unresolved loss. This is massive, catastrophic ambiguous/unresolved loss.

With the repeal of the federal draft and our reliance on an all-volunteer military, the burden of service, grief, and loss has rested on the backs of a small minority of Americans—our active duty and

126

reserve military and their families.

The United States has been at war almost continuously since my birth in the midst of World War II. Many of my relatives and friends served in World War II, Korea, Vietnam, the Cold War, Iraq, Afghanistan, and the "War on Terror." (I may have failed to mention some).

In 1961, while still in high school, I enlisted in the US Navy, and I retired thirty-three years later, in 1994. When someone asks me about my military service, I cheerfully respond, "I had the privilege to advance from seaman to captain in a mere twenty-five years."

Aboard my first submarine, I served alongside WWII submarine sailors. They had survived war patrols in the Pacific and had endured long-term stress and enemy depth charge attacks. That was my first exposure to men with PTSD (combat fatigue/ shell shock, as we called it then). Self-medication and alcoholism were common.

I was in uniform during most of our Vietnam experience. I once shared a hospital room with an Army helicopter pilot who had lost most of his intestines from enemy fire. One of my classmates in submarine school had a metal plate in his head, a Vietnam War casualty from his service as a Navy swift boat captain.

At that time, millions of Americans viewed the Vietnam War as unnecessary, unjust, and immoral, and often blamed the warriors—the thousands of young men who were being drafted and shipped off to fight in the jungles of Vietnam. In the face of widespread public opposition to the war, veterans returned to public anger, shame, and rejection. This compounded their traumatic experience of war and

negatively affected military spouses and children as well. We were
advised not to wear our uniforms off the Navy base or while traveling.

The Wall that Heals

When the mobile Vietnam Memorial exhibit came to my hometown in
2019, it was for me a more moving experience than my visit to the actual memorial wall in Washington, DC. In addition to a smaller replica
of the black granite wall with the names of 58,276 casualties, there was
a large van with videos, pictures of veterans, and memorabilia from
service members.

Two writings among the many on the truck caught my eye. One
was a handwritten letter from a returning soldier. It read in part, "I
came home not to hugs, handshakes, and parades but to jeers, insults,
and protests."

The other was an excerpt from a speech by President Ronald
Reagan at the Vietnam War Memorial in 1988. Reagan said, "Vietnam
service is once more universally recognized as a badge of honor. . . Now
as I see Vietnam veterans take their rightful place among America's
heroes, it appears to me that we have healed. And what can I say to our
Vietnam Veterans, but Welcome Home."

I hope that the wall not only remembers the dead, but also serves to
heal a nation that was once angrily, bitterly, and painfully divided.

During my long Cold War submarine patrols, I and many in my
crew experienced separation, loneliness, and the loss of some of our
shipmates. One of my commanding officers died at age thirty-eight,

leaving behind a wife and three young children.

The physical and emotional scars of war are deep, real, and long-lasting. Following the terrorist attacks on the United States on September 11, 2001, service members and their families were called into combat again. Fortunately, unlike Vietnam, most Americans now embrace our military families and provide them with greater appreciation, recognition, support, and care.

My granddaughter, Katie, studied the war in Vietnam in college. Her assignment was to interview a Vietnam-era veteran. She called me to ask, "Grandpa. What did you do during Vietnam?"

I responded, "Well, Katie, I hid in the North Atlantic."

"Were you afraid?" she asked.

"No, Katie, I was serving aboard a nuclear missile submarine. I was fighting that other war, the Cold War."

Though I did not serve in combat, I did suffer from PTSD. I recovered with the help of medication, therapy, and the grace of God. But I didn't mention those things to Katie that day.

Disease and Death

The Center for Disease Control and Prevention, in their July 2018 report, listed the top-ten leading causes of death in the United States. Accidental death is number three. Suicide is number ten. The other eight are diseases (heart disease, cancer, etc.).

My father died of cancer at fifty-five. My mother succumbed to liver disease (alcoholism). My only sibling died of COPD; she was a lifelong smoker starting at age thirteen. I have outlived my entire family of origin. I often feel like an orphan.

At a young age, I "ran away from home," joined the US Navy, and established my own new Francis family with Linda. Since we lived so far from our birthplaces, Linda and I chose friends as our new family.

Years before Jon was born, Linda and I were members of a small church with a tight-knit group of fellow Christians—in particular, we were part of a group of four families who became our new brothers and sisters, lifelong friends, and grandparents and godparents to our children. We supported each other in our life and faith journeys, gathered together at holidays and birthdays, shared our burdens, mourned our losses, and celebrated our joys and accomplishments.

But now, many of our current friends are widows. I didn't see this coming. One by one, the significant men in my adopted family died of disease.

Don, the surrogate grandfather to our children, was the first to die. John, one of my closest friends ever and the brother I never had, died in 2011. (Read more about John in Part III.) Father Ed, our spiritual leader and my adopted father figure, died in 2014. He was my first spiritual director, a man of immense wisdom and compassion.

These men had sustained, mentored, and supported me for decades. They were part of my life's fabric in joy and in sorrow. It hurts that they are no longer alive. Our circle has inevitably been broken by disease and death.

Within my Irish heritage, we frequently use the term "black

humor." My mother often said, "Life is not for the faint of heart. And we will never get out alive." (You were right, Mom.)

Suicide

According to the National Alliance on Mental Health, suicidal thoughts and behaviors are considered a psychiatric emergency because they are so dangerous—but having such thoughts are not a sign of a personal flaw or a weakness. They are a sign of a person in intense pain. People who try to commit suicide often feel great anguish and hopelessness and see no other way to end the unbearable pain.

Military veterans of wars in Iraq and Afghanistan are choosing suicide at a rate of twenty or more a day.[1] Suicide is the third-leading cause of death among young people, after car accidents and homicide; and death due to opioid overdose is rapidly gaining. According to the Centers for Disease Control and Prevention (CDC), the stress and pain relief qualities of opioids contribute to their misuse and ensuing addiction. Every day in the United States, more than 130 people die of opioid overdoses.[2]

Suicide is one of the most devastating types of loss for those left behind who feel shock, guilt, shame, grief, depression, and denial. We can feel conflicted with feelings of abandonment, rejection, and anger.

---

1 "I survived combat in Iraq and a suicide attempt at home. But many veterans aren't so lucky" by Danny O'Neel, January 16, 2019. *USA TODAY*. See https://www.usatoday.com/story/opinion/voices/2019/01/16/veteran-affairs-suicide-military-iraq-war-column/2580957002/.

2 National Institute on Drug Abuse. January 2019. See https://www.drugabuse.gov/drugs-abuse/opioids/opioid-overdose-crisis.

We are left asking, "Why?"

We may feel as though we should have seen the warning signs, we should have known, we should have prevented it.

Dr. Rando writes that suicide "can contribute to a profound shattering of your self-esteem, with strong feelings of unworthiness, inadequacy, and failure." She stresses that "we are not at fault for someone's suicide. In the end, in the final moment, they made the choice alone."

That knowledge does not prevent our own suffering. We may feel intense guilt, shame, and/or anger that we were not able to prevent the death. Some people feel there is a stigma attached to being associated with a suicide, that others may judge us harshly. Such reactions will impede and delay our own healthy healing if they keep us from seeking help. All the most debilitating bereavement reactions are intensified greatly when the person who completed suicide is your own child.

Rando adds, "The path from brokenness to wholeness is to concentrate all of our energy and focus, not on guilt and anger, but on survival and healing."

Homicide

Blair and Noel provide more wisdom about situations where "someone reached into our life and robbed us of a person we loved."

Our grief response to such a sudden and painful loss is similar to a sudden accidental death, but is much more devastating because we can be so deeply filled with rage.

Survivors may feel some guilt or responsibility as though we feel there might have been something we could have done to prevent the death—or that we were unable to protect our loved one from this violence.

Amidst feelings of unfairness, anger, and guilt—piling grief upon grief—we may also have to navigate the criminal justice system. People whose loved ones were murdered have often said they feel victimized by the criminal justice system, investigators, and the media on top of their own loss, creating "a nearly overwhelming, complicated, and long grief process."

We will all face grief and loss at some point in life—and most likely more than once. For that reason, I have often said that dealing with grief and loss should be taught in school. And now it is. A few years ago, I was invited to speak at a local high school. Ross, the teacher, was also the track and cross-country coach who had known Jon and admired his tenacity and work ethic.

When Ross told me the subjects to be discussed were "Aging, Grief, and Depression," I responded, "I'm your man!" I've become an expert of sorts in all three subjects.

The kids at Ross's high school were in mourning. Two of their classmates had recently been killed in an auto accident while driving to school. In the audience that day were the parents of one of the girls. I greeted the grieving mother and father after my presentation. They thanked me for my presence in their sorrow and said that my words were helpful.

Columbine, Sandy Hook, and Parkland became familiar names like Gettysburg, Pearl Harbor, and 9/11. Schools in the United States have increasingly become places of traumatic loss and mourning with the rise in mass shootings. Twenty years ago the Columbine High School massacre jolted us to the reality that our children are no longer safe in their classrooms. Mental illness, rage, and gun violence know no boundaries. Grief counselors and therapy dogs are becoming common fixtures in American schools. My grandchildren now routinely practice lockdown drills and hide in a janitor's closet.

As a father of a child who died suddenly and violently, I feel particular compassion and kinship with the parents and families who suffer from these preventable tragedies. But anger is my overwhelming default emotion after every school killing in America. I have come to believe that our society has placed our love of guns above our love for our children. Mine is an age-old question—how does a loving God allow evil and chaos to flourish?

I think of my son's lament, "Doesn't God ever intervene anymore?" And that of Professor Wolterstorff, "How is faith to endure, O God, when you allow all this scraping and tearing on us? You have allowed rivers of blood to flow, mountains of suffering to pile up, sobs to become humanity's song . . ."

The sadness and anger inspired by a profound loss can be a powerful motivator for us to take action to make a positive difference in our world. We have the means to prevent many of these tragedies. We can do better.

We must have the will to speak up, rise up, and raise awareness by voicing our concerns to others and sharing our stories.

Takeaways

Remember that it is not a sign of weakness or a flaw to feel depressed or have suicidal thoughts. When feeling overwhelmed, seek help.

Take action as a citizen and human being to focus on raising awareness and seeking solutions to these types of preventable tragedies.

Use wisdom and resolve to voice concerns and share stories.

Recognize and nurture your family relationships, the ties that bind, and embrace your humanness and need to support one another on the journey. Love one another.

"Life is short and we do not have much time to gladden the hearts of those who travel with us. So be swift to love. Make haste to be kind. And go in peace." —Henri-Frédéric Amiel

CHAPTER 11

REINVESTING IN LIFE
(AND RELATIONSHIPS)

I have acknowledged and understand my loss. I am working through my pain, adjusting to the separation from my son, and I have made a sincere commitment to do my grief work. I have created memorials and remembrances to keep Jon "alive." Now what? What's next?

When the idea of going on living is to exist in misery or to heal, I choose to heal. Dr. Therese Rando recommends that the time to heal is when we can "form a new identity." She writes, "Learning to live in the world without our loved one eventually helps us to form a new identity. A piece of ourselves has died. We are forced to see the world with new feelings, thoughts, hopes, expectations, relationships and demands. This takes a long time. As we begin to see and experience the world in a new way, we eventually see ourselves in a new way also."

My life is divided in half. The first half was life with our son. The second half is life without his precious presence. In the early years, some people avoided me altogether. Others greeted me reluctantly with a sad face. The unspoken message was, *You are a victim. You are Jon's grieving father and I struggle to find something to say to you.*

To help relieve what I perceived as the other person's anxiety, I frequently offered a smile and started the conversation.

Later, some people often called me Jon as they greeted me more naturally. I responded, "I'm David. But I have always liked the name Jon."

This became my new identity in a way. I was no longer the pitiful father and victim. I was a champion of Jon's memory and cause.

My new identity and purpose are to keep the lamp burning by reminding people by word and by deed that a young man named Jon Francis once lived joyfully and loved boldly among us.

Reinvesting Emotional Energy

The time came to plant and to look to the future. The emotional energy that I had invested in my important relationship with my son was reinvested in other people and pursuits. Such reinvestment was healthy, rewarding, and necessary to help me resolve my grief and spawn a renewed sense of purpose and meaning in my life. This brought me into contact with the living and with the real world, which furthered my healing.

Rando says, "Deep and painful loss has frequently changed attitudes and perspectives of the bereaved. Those who have loved and lost have reported that their eyes have been opened to new experiences and priorities that were formerly overlooked."

Some of the associated decisions have included making a commitment to living life more fully, appreciating how fragile and precious life is, choosing to finish unfinished business, letting go of anger and guilt and any other emotion that is not adding to my health.

The result is finding new meaning in life. When we pay closer attention to the loved ones we still have with us and be more open to expressing our loving feelings, we become more compassionate. Love is always the answer that will help us accept the help and support of others and be there for them as well. This is a time to love, let go, and let be.

"Needed. A strong, deep person wise enough to allow me to grieve in the depth of who I am, and strong enough to hear my pain without turning away." —Fr. Joe Mahoney

Instead of isolating ourselves in our grief, let's surround ourselves with lovers and helpers, and ask for and accept the presence and help of others. People genuinely care about us and want to provide some comfort and help. On my grief journey, I have identified my circle of helpers.

A Circle of Helpers

My life has forever changed. Life Part II brought unwanted changes in my relationships with family, friends, acquaintances, loved ones, and society.

The stressful or dysfunctional relationships with others in Life Part I became even worse at the start of Life Part II.

I have heard and experienced firsthand that dysfunctional families are often at their worst at holiday gatherings or in a family crisis.

In Life Part II, there is a hole in my heart where Jon once nestled. From my own experience, and that of others, I've learned that grieving well requires that we make the hole smaller. We fill the void by reinvesting our love in others. I invested deep commitment and love in my relationship with my son who nourished me with warmth and joy.

Now I need to open my heart to others. Many people are helping me reinvest: family, spouse, children, grandchildren, old friends and new friends, members of our new club, my faith community, and support group members.

"Members of the Club"
Companion animals
Doctors
Family and friends
Grief counselors
Life coaches
Loved ones
Neighbors
Priests/pastors
Social workers

I learned that the best way I can help my fellow grief travelers is to grieve well myself. I was selfish. I was consumed with my personal grief, the search for Jon, creating the Jon Francis Foundation, and writing about Jon. The expected result: I was ignoring my family and their grief. Fortunately, out of love for me, my youngest daughter, Melissa, energetically reminded me that she was still alive. It was the first of several wake-up calls. Gradually I began to focus a little more attention on my family and fellow grievers.

Three years after Jon's death, I was present at the birth of my sixth grandchild. Our daughter Robin gave birth to a daughter, Camille. I held her shortly after her birth. Camille and I held a lengthy gaze into each other's eyes. She squeezed my finger. I knew it was the start of something beautiful.

Camille turned out to be a gift from God that gently invited me to reinvest my love—like the love for my only son. In the winter of my sorrow, Camille brought me a new spring.

At this writing, Camille is ten years old. We are connected at the hip. I see her nearly every day. We play games and sports. We read. We go skating, sledding, swimming, and bike-riding together. I taught her how to ride her bike and how to play tennis. She fills my heart with joy, love, and gratitude. I am in awe of how a young child could restore my love for life.

Buff

Father Jerry retired and left Ascension Stillwater. A church committee conducted a search for a new head pastor and found Holt Buff Grace. I immediately knew he must be from the South, with a name like Buff. Sure enough, he was from Georgia.

On March 5, in his first year at Ascension, Buff came to our house with a birthday card for Jon. I was blown away by his unexpected and amazing act of kindness and compassion, and his exceptional effort to remember and honor our son. I said to Linda, "I'm going to like this guy."

His very special first act of kindness to our family made a powerful impression. Buff ended up serving for a time as director of the Jon Francis Foundation. As a former Outward Bound instructor, he had massive outdoor knowledge. We called him our "wilderness spiritual director."

Preserving Body, Mind, and Soul

Other grief travelers remind me every day how resilient human beings can be. We can survive and heal from devastating loss and pain.

However, it is not easy and our healing requires effort, hard work, and help from others. While grieving, our emotional life may be unstable and unpredictable. And our physical health can be at risk.

The Reverend Mary Jo Feely leads our Stillwater community of faith in a healing ministry that includes mindfulness and mediation.

I asked her to share her gift here.

Meditation practices are found in many cultures. Some are ancient, going back millennia, while others are newer on the scene. Mediation styles vary greatly, from the silent "Zazen" or seated meditation with Japanese and Chinese roots, to the more recent practices of mindfulness adapted from traditional Buddhist practices and what is known as

Centering Prayer, a Christian meditation practice developed by Fr. Thomas Keating with an emphasis on inner silence.

Over the past few decades, mindfulness practices have grown in popularity, thanks in part to the ground-breaking Mindfulness-Based Stress Reduction (MBSR) work developed by Jon Kabat-Zinn in 1979. Kabat-Zinn, an internationally known meditation teacher, author, clinician and researcher in the fields of mind/body and integrative medicine, is an expert in stress reduction and the health-related benefits of mindfulness meditation in supporting one to deal with illness, pain, and stress.

Henry Emmons is an integrative psychiatrist who incorporates the practice of mindfulness in his clinical work. Dr. Emmons is the author of *The Chemistry of Joy* and *The Chemistry of Calm*, which address the powerful healing benefits of meditation techniques in the treatment of depression and anxiety. Additionally, meditation practices are finding their way into corporate businesses and schools as well.

—Reverend Mary Jo Feely

Early in my grief journey, I gave no thought to the care of my body or my mind. I used all of the energy and strength I had in order to power through the daily tasks I was driven to complete.

Many years after we recovered Jon's body and laid him to rest, I began to recognize how messed up I was. That's when I began the reconstruction work on my body and mind.

My friend, Father Jerry, encouraged me to join him in his yoga class. For most of my life, I thought yoga was weird. *Real* exercise was running long distances and lifting heavy weights! Now I am a convert. Yoga turned out to be the right combination of body conditioning and mind healing. My personal experience tells me that yoga has many benefits in our recovery from loss, including meditation.

My twenty-five-year running career ended after my first and last marathon in 2003. My legs were beat up. So I took up biking. Biking is excellent physical conditioning, gets me outdoors, and supports my mental health with the stimulating feeling of nature, freedom, and adventure. In addition, there are many valid studies confirming the mental and physical health benefits of being in nature (hiking, camping, fishing, walking, biking, running).

My wife Linda and I take walks together. During the cold Minnesota winter, we walk on the indoor track at Stillwater High School. That activity has two benefits: 1) the exercise, and 2) being present in a building that was an important part of Jon's life, joy, and development.

Engaging in physical activities and outdoor experiences promote mental and emotional revitalization, and they help to reduce feelings of tension, confusion, anger, and depression. Walking outdoors is almost as good physical activity as a run. I frequently walk to the cemetery.

David Francis visited his son's gravesite at the Rutherford Cemetery near Stillwater. "I come here often to speak with Jon," he said last week. "It's often like a mantra: I miss you, I love you. It's a place of

peace and connection. It's hard, but he assures me that he's fine."
David Francis of Stillwater fought to find his son Jon, and now he's
helping other families of missing adults.

—Kevin Giles, *Minneapolis Star Tribune*, May 27, 2010

You may recall that I suffered from both depression and PTSD. If
left untreated, mental trauma can be crippling. I sought medical
intervention and was prescribed an antidepressant. It adjusted my brain
chemistry and allowed me to heal.

The brain trauma was more challenging. I delayed grief therapy too
long. I regret not getting help earlier. Exploring, understanding,
confronting, and addressing the mental damage that deep grief caused
me was invaluable. Talk therapy using cognitive-behavioral therapy
(CBT) and dialectical behavior therapy (DBT) were critical in my
healing. I recommend it!

Frequently we mask our grief and dull our pain with drugs,
narcotics, and alcohol. I witnessed this for most of my life. I grew up in
an alcoholic family and served in a navy and a high technology industry
that was often addicted. Hiding from our pain in a chemical fog will
delay, prolong, and sabotage our grief work. Worse yet, addiction
messes up your life, career, and relationships—the perfect way to add
insult to injury.

In my own family, I have seen the benefits of treatment and family,
professional, and community support. We have come a long way in
understanding and treating substance abuse, addiction, and alcoholism.

Like most body or mind diseases, help is available and effective. Use it!

The Standard American Diet, appropriately abbreviated, SAD, is composed of lots of sugar, white flour, starches, and meats. This was my preferred diet until recently. My annual physical examination this year uncovered my high cholesterol. My free ride was over!

With the help of my wife, who is an amazing cook, I went on the healthier Mediterranean diet. Of course, I wish I had developed the discipline to do this earlier. However, I consider this a late but important step in self-care: taking care of my aging body.

I live with many regrets: *I wish I had . . . I should have . . .* They linger, and they are nagging. Like countless other men, I was committed to my career. I worked hard over long hours and lots of business travel to provide safety, security, and status for my family and, of course, myself. Since I grew up in an environment of scarcity, I was driven to succeed financially.

I missed many hours, days, special events, quiet times, talks, meals, and recreation with my family. I frequently think of the cartoon picturing a man on his deathbed with the caption: "I wish I had spent more time at the office."

I have no resolution. Yet I was arrogant enough to sit down and write a self-help book. Still I haven't found, and I do not have, an answer for the recurring guilt I feel for being an absentee husband and father.

One of my lingering regrets since Jon's death is that I had very few conversations with him about religion. He majored in religion in college, was a youth minister, and (as I only learned during one of my book readings at a Lutheran church in Idaho) he was regarded as an emerging theologian knowledgeable about Christianity in its many denominations. While living in Utah, Jon was studying Mormonism.

In reality, if I did not believe in eternal life, I would go mad. If I did not believe that Jon is now in heaven discussing religion with God, I would be inconsolable. My faith is shaken but not lost.

During six of the nine years that Jon played soccer, I was his coach. I had never played soccer, so I worked hard to be a good coach. At age fifty, I attended several weeks of coach's school and earned my D License. I triumphantly presented my certificate to Jon. "Hey, Jon," I said, "I passed, and I now qualify to coach soccer at the high school level." He thought for a moment and responded, "Dad, that's a scary thought."

Coaching Jon's youth soccer team was one of the most rewarding and enjoyable experiences in my life. Unfortunately, In addition to Linda and me, three sets of "my soccer parents" would eventually, tragically loose a son. Jared died in an auto accident. His parents, Jim and Gayle, were positive and encouraging. Chris's older brother, Greg, died in an avalanche. His parents, Dan and Sue, were very kind and supportive. Dan writes about his son Greg's, death in Part III.

Nick's parents, Bill and Noel, always raised my spirits. Nick committed suicide. Bill contacted me and shared information with me about a faith-based, grief program he and his wife Noel had attended

146

after their son's death. Bill gently encouraged me to sign up.

I participated in a 13-week GriefShare group. I found it helpful. The grief-and-loss therapy was solid. The theology had a Southern Baptist Christian flavor, and the motivation to read and interpret scripture was enlightening.

I recommend GriefShare as part of a healing process. It addresses the crisis of faith and the struggle to answer the question: Where was God? See Grief Resources at the end of this book for more information about GriefShare.

Takeaways

There's a time for every purpose under heaven:

"To everything there is a season, and a time to every purpose under the heaven: A time to be born, and a time to die; a time to plant, and a time to pluck up that which is planted; A time to kill, and a time to heal; a time to break down, and a time to build up; A time to weep, and a time to laugh; a time to mourn, and a time to dance; A time to cast away stones, and a time to gather stones together; a time to embrace, and a time to refrain from embracing; A time to get, and a time to lose; a time to keep, and a time to cast away; A time to rend, and a time to sew; a time to keep silence, and a time to speak; A time to love, and a time to hate; a time of war, and a time of peace. . ."

—Ecclesiastes 3:1–8 (KJV)

Yoga, mindfulness, and meditation can improve mental and physical health.

Take care of yourself, body, mind, and spirit.

Reinvest your love.

CHAPTER 12

LIVING AND LOVING AGAIN AFTER LOSS

Linda reminded me of the countless acts of kindness we received from hundreds of people who supported us in our suffering and helped us find Jon. She said, "God is in the faces, hearts, hands, and feet of others." I asked her to add her thoughts here.

From the beginning, and over the years since Jon's accident, I have felt the presence of God in the people God sent to help us. Time after time, since July 15, 2006, people came to us to offer their support.

I remember a young woman with her two young sons, who drove for four hours from Boise, Idaho, to be with us in Stanley. With her long golden curls, she appeared to me like an angel. She stayed most of the day and helped take down the tent we set up for our grandchildren —Audrey and Charlie. People came from so many places and from so far away. That was God in human skin.

The impact of Jon's accident has made me more aware and attuned to others who are going through similar suffering. I pay greater attention now when I hear news of a lost child or missing person.

Through our foundation, I hope to help others struggling with grief, despair, and unresolved loss caused by a missing loved one.

Helping others may be the best help we can give ourselves.

My family is making a slow recovery. Our lives are changed forever. There are many activities I may never do again—like sending Christmas cards. They have lost their importance, take great effort, and cause great stress. I might tackle it again someday. There are places I may never visit again. Every time I visit a familiar place, or a new place, or do a new activity, I long to have Jon with me, to share with him the wonders of life. Living is bittersweet now.

Our three daughters are focusing on their own families, jobs, and lives again. For a long time it was hard to figure out where we wanted to be or what we should do. Nothing was right. Nothing fit. Slowly the rhythm of life pulled us back to a nearly normal routine and focus. We began to function again.

I will always have an empty place where Jon belongs. I will always miss him. But I'm convinced that I will see him again.

The challenge for me is to discover my new relationship with Jon and with others as I move forward on this new, un-chosen path I must take. Life continues with joys and with sorrows—our children and grandchildren; the birth of a new granddaughter, Camille; the illnesses of friends and loved ones; the rhythm of daily life. The difference now is that sorrow is a constant. Joy is welcomed, but often elusive. Life continues. We move forward. —Linda

Linda has been diligent in doing her grief work. I lag behind. I look to her wisdom. She is and has always been the glue that holds our family together.

Robin left New York and returned to Minnesota to be closer to her family, bringing us a lovely gift, Camille. Doug, Jocelyn, and their two children continue to live in Idaho. Jocelyn says she feels closer to Jon there. Melissa and Steve remain in Minnesota. Four of our six grandchildren live nearby.

Grandchildren are so much fun; I recommend having them first.

Grieving Well

Of the many authors who have written about grief and loss, one stands out to me. The Reverend Dr. Alla Renée Bozarth, author of *Life is Hello Life is Goodbye: Grieving Well Through All Kinds of Loss* is an Episcopal priest, a grief therapist, and a poet. I found her book to be the most uplifting. It is an inspiring mix of grief counseling, spirituality, and poetry. Her message to Linda and me after Jon's death remains one of the most meaningful and comforting I have ever received.

Alla reminds us that, "Grief is a passion to endure. People can be stricken with it, victims of it, stuck in it. Or they may meet it, get through it, and become quiet victors through the active, honest, and courageous process of grieving."

That is our goal. That is the Holy Grail. We will no longer be victims of grief. We will be victors over it.

Alla shares from Chapter 12, *Essentials of the Art of Grieving*:

"On the other side of grief we can discover the joy and gratitude that come with new and renewed zest." [Yes, *zest.*] "I can decide to

151

teach myself through suffering. I can teach myself to become more human and loving . . ."

"Living through desperation and despair with courage and honesty can prepare us to be more understanding and compassionate toward ourselves and others . . ."

"In deep grief, someone wrote [to Alla], 'I now have a hole in my heart where the sorrow of the world flows in.' Sorrow can teach us compassion."

"Above all, through loss experiences we can teach ourselves a new kind of joy—one which is large enough to contain our pain and to transform it into a new kind of power, the power to make us whole."

"Trust yourself. Trust your feelings. Own your feelings; recognize them as *your own*. Feel your feelings. They won't destroy you, because you can learn to express them safely and constructively with the reassuring help of others."

"Care for yourself. If your own biological family is not supporting you, you can adopt persons whom you trust to be family for you, to give you the nourishing support you need . . ."

"Allow yourself to suffer your own healing process, to suffer your own meaning. You need to discover what the loss *means* to you and what healing means as well. Let it take as long as it takes."

"The greater the loss, the longer your recovery will be. The more meaning, the more of yourself, the more life and time still go into the healing."

"Take as long or as short a time as you need. Become an active agent in your life again. You can do what you need to do to be healed."

Granger Westberg asserted, "Life will never be the same. However, we begin to realize that we need not fear life. We can live it again. We can even love it again. Not everything has been taken from us. Life can be affirmed."

I have learned that grief work is hard work that takes resilience, energy, and a personal commitment. In order to grieve well, I needed to take personal responsibility for my healing and walk the walk.

Others helped me, of course. But my journey was my journey.

Some Thoughts and Prayers for Healing

"Thoughts and Prayers" sounds like a brand for a greeting card company. How many times have you heard someone say, "My thoughts and prayers are with you"?

It's common, and perhaps it has reached the level of cliché. It's not that people don't genuinely care or recognize our loss. To me it shows the struggle and difficulty in our culture to find the right "grief words" and to communicate compassionately with others.

Throughout my grief travels, I have found some "thoughts and prayers" and words of healing and wisdom from various sources that I offer to you.

To begin, I include here again with her permission, a poem by Reverend Mary Farr that she graciously allowed to be included with the Foreword for this book. Her book in the form of a poem, *If I Could Mend Your Heart*, is not only beautiful writing, but it also beautifully describes the stages of grief. I regard it as poetic healing.

I have added corresponding summary comments in brackets.

If I Could Mend Your Heart . . . I would weave together the ragged edges of your threadbare heart and soothe your pain your shock and disbelief.

[In grief, we experience shock and denial]

I would invite you to touch your sorrow and feel your feelings and not pretend to be strong or capable or composed.

[Trust your feelings and allow yourself to feel them. Your feelings cannot destroy you.]

I would listen without comment, to all that is unsettled in your soul, your doubts, your anger, your fears about the future.

[Express your fears, sadness, and hurt safely with others. Choose and adopt a circle of helpers, a family you choose, so you can receive support.]

I would heed your cries and probing questions. What might you have done wrong or, what you might not have done at all.

[Guilt is a strong emotion. Grief travelers ruminate over all past

*interactions—thinking of the "if onlys" and often feeling guilty and
responsible for the loss.]*

For more than a single ending, your loss may spark other sorrows, other
conclusions, good-byes, and thorny adjustments in every corner of your
soul.

*[Remember a lost loved one realistically with their positive and their
negative qualities in order to hold onto the person in a healthy way—so you
are not prevented from living your own life.]*

If I could mend your heart . . . I would promise not to say, "Look how
well you're handling things," or, "Cheer up. God wouldn't give you
more than you could handle," or, "You'll be over this soon."

*[Recognize that when others try to help, they may not say helpful things.
They may feel helpless and awkward. Have low expectations about the
ability of others to comfort us especially early in our grief.]*

Instead, I would whisper in your ear, "We live in a fragile and imperfect
world tinged by brokenness and cloaked in unanswered questions.
Some things truly aren't fair. This is hard."

*[Sharp pain is undeniable. If we focus on the unfairness of the loss, we
will redirect our grief to anger and rage.]*

For I don't think loss is about "handling things well," or "keeping it all
together." But about keeping afloat in a rising tide of doubt. Asking the
silence, "Why?"

155

[We struggle to understand why the loss happened. What is the divine plan in this? Questioning is normal, but also listen and pray and receive.]

"What is the meaning of this?" It's about learning to co-exist with an unwanted visitor, with alien thoughts, and depleted spirits.

[Grief over a significant loss can never be completely resolved. Resolution of any kind comes through continuing with our "grief work." Closure is for bank accounts—not for love accounts.]

If I could mend your heart . . . I would draw you a plan and perfect map to light your path from confusion and despair to a place of new tomorrows and rewarding journeys.

[There is no Standard Operating Procedure to guide us through grief. "Time does not heal. Prayer heals. The Holy Spirit Heals. You choose to heal!]

A place where anger could release its grip on understanding, and anxiousness might speak to acceptance.

[Grief is a passion we must endure. We can be a victim of it, be stuck in it, or we can face it, go through it, and be quietly victorious with honest and courageous grieving.]

I would shape for you a fresh way of seeing, through prisms of sunlight.

[When the choice is misery or healing, Choose to heal. Learn to live without our loved one helps us form a new identity and see the world with different expectations. But this takes a long time. Seeing and experiencing the world in a new way helps us see ourselves in new ways.]

Prisms of sunlight that temper your pain with compassion and replace your doubts with faith, your grief with gratitude, your fear with trust.

[Joy and gratitude can emerge on the other side of grief—even a new zest for life. We can decide to learn through our suffering and become more human and loving.]

If I could mend your heart . . . I would open wide the doors of renewed hope a hope much larger than wishes. One that waits, patiently, willingly, expectantly . . .

[Even though life will never be the same, we can live and love again. We have not lost everything.]

This fresh hope I send would let you step up with courage to the new day, trusting that even pain can be transformed.

[Loss, desperation, and despair, when faced with courage and honesty can help us be more understanding and compassionate and discover a new kind of joy that can transform our pain and make us whole.]

If I could mend your heart . . . I would lead you by the hand to this place of healing so that you might once again walk in your own path and make memories.

[Painful loss can change us in many ways and open us to new experiences.]

I would share with you a secret—Joy is not about music and dance and laughter, but about the acceptance of Life.

[That is our Holy Grail. We will be victorious over grief. Seeing the world in a new way helps us see ourselves in new ways.]

Healing happens only where fear and love, joy and sorrow, tears and smiles can forge a lasting peace.

[Great joy, laughter, and amazement comes with open loving hearts. Love wins.]

The healing I speak of lies not in some safe place along the way, but in having made the journey stage by stage.

[Grieving is a personal process, with no time limit, and no "right" way to do it. We can travel through the stages of grieving: accept the loss, process the pain of grief, adjust without the deceased, and live effectively in the world despite our loss.]

Until you reach that place, a place you may not now believe exists, I will save your space, and watch with confidence *for your smiles yet to be.*

[God is love. I bless you; I release you. I set you free; I set me free. I let you be; I let me be.]

~

"Yea, though I walk through the valley of the shadow of death, I will fear no evil: for thou art with me; thy rod and thy staff they comfort me." —Psalm 23.4 (KJV)

"Those who sow with tears will reap with songs of joy. Those who go out weeping, carrying seed to sow, will return with songs of joy, carrying sheaves with them." —Psalm 126: 5–6 (ESV)

"O Great Spirit, Whose voice I hear in the winds, and whose breath gives life to the whole world, hear me! I am small and weak. I need your strength and wisdom." —Native American Prayer

"Great Spirit, now I pray to you . . . Great Spirit, hear me: My soul is weary. Now I pray that your spirit will dwell in me." —Kiowa prayer

"Never forget that you are not alone. The Divine is with you, helping and guiding. He is the companion who never fails, the friend whose love comforts and strengthens. Have faith . . ." —Sri Arubindo

"I offer you peace. I offer you love. I offer you friendship. I see your beauty. I hear your need. I feel your feelings. My wisdom flows from the Highest Source. I salute that Source in you. Let us work together for unity and love." —Mahatma Gandhi

"O Lord you are the Giver of life, Remover of pains and sorrows, Bestower of happiness. May we receive the supreme sin-destroying light of the Creator of the universe. May You guide our intellect in the right direction." —Hindu Haven mantra

"Verily, with every difficulty there is relief. Verily, with every difficulty there is relief." —Qur'an 94:5–6

"The wound is the place where the light enters you." —Rumi

"It is nonsense to say that God fills the gap; He does not fill it, But keeps it empty so that our communion with another may be kept alive. Even at the cost of pain." —Dietrich Bonhoeffer

"Our load is heavy. But we will get stronger even though the load weighs the same." —Kim Owen Mazur

"Grief dares us to love once more." —Terry Tempest Williams

"Grief is exhausting and requires the strength of an Olympic athlete." —Joyce Carol Oates

"Lord, I come before you today in need of your healing hand. In you all things are possible. Hold my heart within yours, and renew my mind, body, and soul. I am lost, but I come to you with grace. You gave us life, and you also give us the gift of infinite joy. Give me the strength to move forward on the path you've laid out for me. Guide me towards better health, and give me the wisdom to identify those you've placed around me to help me get better. Amen." —Catholic Prayer

"O Lord, only you know how hard life has been for me. Only you have seen each moment of my day and night. Only you feel my pain and understand my discomfort. Only you are beside me through my grief and sorrow. Only you have been within each moment to comfort me. O Lord, break through the loneliness of my suffering. You have encountered sorrow and laid a glorious path of hope, healing and the promise of heaven in my heart. Amen. —Healing Prayer, St. Peter's Anglican Church, Oshawa

For you shall go out in joy, and be led back in peace; the mountains and the hills before you shall burst into song, and all the trees of the field shall clap their hands." —Isaiah 55:12

"The LORD bless you and keep you; The LORD make His face shine upon you, and be gracious to you; The LORD lift up His countenance upon you, And give you peace." —Numbers 6:24–26 (NKJV)

"Life is short and we do not have much time to gladden the hearts of those who travel with us. So be swift to love. Make haste to be kind. And go in peace." —Henri-Frédéric Amiel (this one is so good, it deserves repeating from a Takeaway!)

Some Deaths You Never Get Over

Easter and All Souls Days are Every Day—

Fall comes

and you remember—

Winter comes

and you remember—

Spring comes

and you remember—

Summer comes

and you remember—

The thousand moments

of sharing the same

dimensions, meanings

and memories.

The heart beats

through the seasons,

each one in rhythm

with the Beloved's Name,

because you know

that to remember is to honor

and to continue to live and be able

to pass love forward in your own name.

You do not need to get over the loss.

You need to incorporate what came before

and the meaning of loss into your ongoing

life and the love you live out—until

memory will no longer be needed,

because you are together again

and healed of the need for memory

in all at once everywhere Now.

—Alla Renée Bozarth, from *Love's Alchemy* ©2014.

Takeaways

You are not alone, and you don't need to suffer alone.

Share your story and listen to the stories of others.

Grief work is hard work. It takes resilience, energy, and a personal commitment. Others can help.

But our journey is our journey.

PART III

FELLOW GRIEF TRAVELERS

Since our son died, I have been much more aware and sensitive to the grief of others who have lost loved ones. Though Linda and I are particularly alert to the tragic stories about missing persons, we have come to know many who are grieving those who died from other causes. Many grief travelers have joined our circle over the past fourteen years. More will join in the future.

I asked several of my fellow grievers to contribute to this book. I asked each to describe their loss and pain and talk about their journey through the valley. Here are their stories of love, loss, and learning.

CHAPTER 13

BETHANY
By her mother, Kim

David speaks:

I met Kim at a GriefShare meeting. I was one of two men in the group populated with many women, mostly widows. They spoke about the grief widows know when they are abruptly alone after countless years in a partnership, loving and caring for (or tolerating) a husband.

Kim stood out. She was not a widow. She was a mother in agony. I sat in disbelief as she described the recent sudden, accidental death of her middle daughter, Bethany. I would learn that her burden was beyond measure because, in addition, her oldest daughter had a grim diagnosis of brain cancer. During our time together, I grew in admiration for her steadfastness and courage. I developed a profound respect for the way she was coping with her grief through her art.

Each week Kim showed us new pages in her "grief coloring book." I expressed my appreciation and encouraged her to continue to draw, to write, and to find a publisher. I was delighted and honored when I received her creative and exceptional book, *Losing My Reflection: a grief journal coloring book by Kim Mazur.*

Kim speaks:

My name is Kim. My husband Mike and I married in 1982. We met in college. I studied speech pathology at Indiana State University, and Mike studied mechanical engineering at Rose-Hulman Institute of Technology. Upon graduation, Mike took a job with 3M Company in Minnesota. As of now, we have moved nine times during our thirty-six-year marriage.

I am creative and artistic. Mike is logical and mathematical (a typical engineer). I enjoy creating props for the shows at our local community theater, The Phipps Center for the Arts, dressing the sets and creating the illusion of the time and locale in which the play takes place.

I feel blessed to be Mike's wife. He is very smart and hardworking in his job and at home. He loves math and uses it to analyze nearly everything. Mike thinks things through and finds the best solution in any given situation. He seeks the best in all things, including himself, looks for the best in others, and is quick to support them. He is kind, loving, and supportive of me and my crazy adventures. And he is kinda cute! What more could I ask for from a partner in life?

We were blessed with three wonderful and caring daughters each as different from one another as night is from day. Jessica, our oldest, is prayerful, quiet, reflective, gentle, and kind. Kayla, our youngest, is funny and spontaneous, and she enjoys a practical joke now and then. She is stubborn and quick to stand up for what she believes in.

Bethany was our middle daughter. We shared a love of cooking, and we both had an artistic and creative side. She was caring, strong-minded, and she fought with passion for whom and what she believed in. She was the person you wanted on your team. She did not give up or in when her mind was made up. She was athletic, smart, artistic, and good at nearly everything she did. She loved rugby and played tight end for several seasons at the University of Wisconsin River Falls. I think she loved the songs and the parties afterward the most.

Her first passion was competitive cheerleading, an interest that taught her hard work and focus and took her all around the East Coast and to several other countries. She cheered for a year at Iowa State University. She was truly good at so many things, it was hard for her to decide on a college major. She "found herself" after meeting a handsome guy in a bar and bought him a shot. Joel became her best friend and helped her find the focus she was seeking in her life. They set up a household and she went on to earn a degree in agricultural engineering.

Bethany was excited to marry Joel, and they began planning their wedding. She chose sunflowers for the celebration—a favorite she shared with my father with whom Bethany had a strong connection. He told everyone at a party on the night I went into labor with her that he would be a grandfather again the following morning at 7:30. Bethany was born at 7:33! Her birth was the only one he predicted.

Mike and I were with friends at a wedding reception the afternoon of July 18, 2015. I was excited to tell Bethany about the wedding venue; I thought it would be perfect for her wedding. About thirty minutes into the reception, Mike stepped away from our table to answer his cellphone, which was not unusual since it happened often with his job.

Within minutes, Mike returned and asked me to go outside and take a walk. He said that Joel called. Bethany had a car accident on the road alongside their home. She died in their back yard.

I could not believe what I was hearing. It took my breath away. I kept thinking, *Mike that is not funny!* I wanted it to be a joke. But this wasn't something he would joke about. I tried to hide my emotions as we walked back into the reception to tell our friends we were leaving. But everyone knew something awful had occurred by the look of terror on my face.

My grief journey had begun. From that moment, I was changed. I had lost part of my identity, a part of who I was. I lost that connection with the present and future with my precious daughter. I mourned over what SHOULD have been. When I saw my reflection in the mirror, I did not know who that person was anymore. I was a stranger to myself. And I feared losing Joel as well. Over their five-year relationship, Joel had become family, he was already my son-in-law. We didn't need a legal piece of paper; I loved him and continue to love him as if he were my own son. As time keeps marching on, I learn more and more about why she fell in love with him.

Joel was walking to their mailbox when he heard the crash. He was the first on the scene and called 911. He pulled Bethany out of her car and started CPR. The EMTs arrived and took over. But they couldn't save her. Joel was horrified that he could not save Bethany's life; but there was nothing he could have done.

The coroner's report said Bethany died on impact.

I struggle to describe how deeply I hurt. No words adequately express the emptiness I felt every day. I was desperate to find that magic formula to make this ache go away. I did not want to feel this way for the rest of my life. I knew I needed to do something.

In my search, I found a group called The Compassionate Friends (TCF). The TCF focus is specific to the loss of a child. There are chapters all over the world facilitated by other parents who have lost children. I found comfort in being able to talk about Bethany and knowing it was okay to cry. Everyone there "got it" because they were living the same life change. My family has attended two of the national conferences, and we plan to attend more. Strange as it may sound, there is comfort in being surrounded by 1,500 people who get it and live it. The speakers are great and the workshops abundant and helpful.

The first Thanksgiving was hard. I waited for Bethany to walk through the front door and throw her arms around each person in her typical big bear hug. When I mentioned her in conversation, family would politely listen then change the subject. She was the elephant in the room. That made me angry and cut my heart like a knife.

I felt sad when I saw other people laugh, because I didn't remember how. I wanted to feel happiness again, I wanted to laugh again. I envy family and friends who still have a whole functioning family. They can't wait for their children to visit. One of mine will never visit again. When those feelings rise, I have to walk away because I don't want my unfathomable sadness to take away from their joy. Don't get me wrong, my heart is overjoyed for them, but for me it makes my loss all the more apparent.

I am not angry with God because I refuse to believe that a loving God would take away a loved one and cause pain and sickness. I do wonder how "God's plan" and our freedom to make choices work together. I believe that our souls are here to learn and grow, and we need both darkness and light and pain and goodness to grow and learn.

I still struggle with waves of grief from missing my child. I still want her to walk in the door and throw her arms around me and say, "I love you mama," as if she were claiming me. I still have days when I feel alone in a crowd. I do not feel that the pain has lessened even slightly, although I do feel as time goes on that I am learning to adjust to this new life. It's not a life I would choose for anyone.

I met David Francis at a GriefShare group. At GriefShare, David found some comfort in the scriptures that were tied to each of the lessons, but I am not there yet. GriefShare had some good information, but I did not agree with some of their interpretations of how to grieve properly, which were not necessarily tied to a particular Bible passage.

My burden is made heavier by the sorrow and sense of foreboding that I will suffer the death of another child. Our firstborn daughter, Jessica, has brain cancer. In April 2015, three months before Bethany died, we learned that Jessica's cancer was a grade 3 anaplastic astrocytoma. She began having debilitating nerve pain that would come and go. As it increased, she was unable to control it and her anxiety attacks began. The week of Bethany's funeral and for months after,

I sat with Jessica in the Emergency Room as she was in full-blown anxiety attacks. I felt helpless; this was yet another thing I could not fix. Moms fix their children's scraped knees and bumped heads. I could not make Jessica's cancer go away. Nor could I bring Bethany back. I'd asked Bethany to help me through this, to help me help Jessica—be my strength and sounding board. I was counting on her to keep me strong, but she was gone.

Jessica's cancer is now a grade 4 glioblastoma. I watch her slip away a little at a time. I watched her lose her hair. She is losing the ability to walk without assistance. Her left arm is atrophying, and the chemo seems to affect her thinking, some days clouding it. Jessica is such a sweet, gentle soul. I wonder how I will survive with two of my kids in heaven, and this makes me angry. I don't know which is worse—losing a child suddenly, without warning, or watching one slowly slip away. I worry daily about my youngest daughter, Kayla. I have to fight a feeling of panic when she does not answer her phone right away.

What has surprised me since losing Bethany is how many others have lost a child—people I went to school with, people I volunteer with, and many I never knew before our loss. It is a deep and silent pain that is not talked about, almost like cancer was years ago.

Loss is a subject that people just don't talk about. Death is that elephant in the room, people do not know what to say or how to react. What do you say?

I think I am a better person now as a result of this tremendous loss, although I wish there had been an easier way to arrive at this point. I am more compassionate. I now know that grief does not end but changes with time. Sometimes our pain changes; sometimes our pain changes us. I now know that grief goes on far past the days when a casserole was dropped off or the sympathy cards stopped arriving.

I want people to talk about Bethany and to ask about Bethany. I will not become sadder when someone brings her up. Talking about her does not make it worse. I am already sad. I am fully aware every day that she is gone. Talking about her is actually a very important part of the healing process. When people ask about her, tell stories about her, or share a "sign," it makes my heart sing. It makes me happy that she is still in people's hearts and minds. I NEED to hear about these things.

When people share these memories or moments, I save them or print out a copy so when I have one of my bad days or moments I can go to them, remember her, and feel her presence.

I am learning to listen to the intent of people's words, not the words themselves. Sometimes people say things that are hurtful:

"God needed another angel."

"Only the good die young."

"You are so strong."

"I could not do what you are doing."

"She is in a better place"

I find comfort while reading about near-death experiences. The one common thread such people share from their experience is the way they describe the place (heaven) on the other side of physical life. Love. It's that simple. LOVE.

David asked me to share what I have learned so far. This is what I have learned: Your love is unique, and so is your grief. The way you are grieving is the right way for you. No one can truly tell you how to navigate your grief process. For me, there are no 1-2-3 steps. The steps are all over the place in no particular order, and the steps often repeat themselves. We understand grief only to the extent by which we have experienced it.

The love, care, and acts of compassion and kindness from my theater friends and those in my community and many others have helped me survive and move forward. I want others to know how much people in grief depend on and appreciate acts of kindness. During my most vulnerable time and days of disbelief, having others "be there" in simple ways was food for my broken heart.

Writing this chapter has given me an opportunity to thank so many who have been "there" for me:

Kim Mahoney Barrio flew from Illinois to sing and support our family. She gave me the book she found left behind in the airplane seat pocket. The book is *Heaven Is For Real*. Kim lost a daughter. She is a fellow grieving mother.

Kasey Tunell made phone calls, arranged food, and so much more. Cheryl Solberg, who lost her son, helped because she too understands. My Aunt Sara Abendroth, a hospice worker, sends me notes of encouragement. My cousin Lisa Gronberg is a grieving mother who understands. Mark and Linda Triplet, people I met through TCL, are examples of living after loss. Jan Flowers sent me an ornament with a butterfly in it. A neighbor, who succeeded in remaining anonymous, left a copy of *Chicken Soup for Grieving Souls* in our mailbox.

Debbie Miller is always willing to listen and let me cry. Mary Bjerke gave me books on grieving. I will read them, I promise.

Mark Koski and Mark Sturino, "theater family" and big brothers, are an ever-loving presence. My dear friend Peggy Gastineau, who knows the pain of loss, calls me always at just the right time.

My mom understands my pain and listens. And Mike is my rock, my defender, my protector, my husband.

I am grateful to all of the people who have come forward to share the pain of their loss, a loss I did not know about until Bethany's death.

Finding others who understand, who get it, has been the most helpful. They do not want to fix you because they know you can't be fixed. They know you will never be your "old self." They know you will have good moments and weepy moments, and that is okay. We are free to talk about our child (or loved one) in their presence.

I always say, I *have* a child—not I *had* a child. Writing and drawing about grief were important steps for me in my grief journey.

Creating my grief coloring book, *Losing My Reflection,* was an act of love for Bethany. The Dedication: "To Bethany, whose death inspired this book."

David adds:
Sadly, Kim's daughter Jessica died in September 2019.

CHAPTER 14

BIL "IT IS WHAT IT IS"
by Megan

David speaks:

I've known Megan since she was a young girl just out of high school. She was the younger daughter of our close friends, Don and Sally Caldwell. Linda and I saw Megan at church, family gatherings, and celebrations. We watched her grow into a wonderful woman. We were not surprised that she chose a helping profession, occupational therapy.

When I first saw the name Bil Gangl on a Caldwell family Christmas letter, my first impression was, "He's missing some letters. Bill has two L's, not one. And Gangl is missing an *e* and the second *g*. But what Bil was not missing was outstanding character and commitment.

Bil was a dedicated and skilled teacher, coach, husband, and father. I saw that all who knew him (family, friends, students, athletes, and his peers) held Bil in deep affection. He made Megan happy and together they raised two awesome children.

It happens much too often. I attend a funeral, listen to the eulogies, and think, *boy, I wish I had known him better*. I sure wish I had known Bil better and spent much more time with him.

175

Megan writes:

I met Bil through mutual friends and was intrigued from our first conversation. I knew I wanted to be with someone who was engaging and creative, always willing to jump in and try new things, and honest and trustworthy to the core. Bil was all those things and more. We married after dating two-and-a-half years, and then built our life together, including rewarding careers, two children, and many enjoyable activities.

Bil had charisma and was willing to speak up for what he thought was right. He was a natural leader. He was funny too! He was known for telling bad jokes and great stories. These traits attracted people to him—whether at home, in his work, or even at a wayside rest when we traveled across country.

Many people refer to their spouse as a soul mate. I think this was true for Bil and me. When he died, I felt that half of me died along with him.

"It is what it is," was one of Bil's quotes after his diagnosis with terminal cancer. He was almost fifty years old, and both of our children were in college. We were looking forward to the final launching of our children into adulthood, and time with each other as empty nesters. But it was not to be.

When Bil was first diagnosed, we were both angry and sad at the same time. Afterward, Bil said, "It is what it is." That attitude and acceptance helped us live with the cancer instead of wasting our energy asking, "Why me?" or "Why now?" Together we committed to focus instead on living each day and every possible day in the future.

He survived the cancer for two-and-a half years, quite an accomplishment for his type of cancer, but he died way before his time. He had many more years to teach, be a grandparent, relax in retirement, and do more good for others. He was an accomplished and respected middle school teacher, a wonderful father, son, brother, and a great husband.

I decided to use a question and answer approach to list frequently asked questions about grief and loss and describe how I have coped after Bil died. I asked many questions of others and myself as I was grieving, and I still do today.

After I became more stable and comfortable in my new life, I began reaching out to others who were newly widowed. I became a sounding board, providing support as they sorted out their new lives. In all my conversations, I found it helpful to hear other opinions or share my own, but the decision of how to proceed was left to the other person.

Several of my widow and widower friends shared their experiences about how they managed, so I have included their ideas and wisdom as well. I have found no hard and fast rules, or right or wrong methods, but I did find ways that helped me work through my grieving.

Question: What support did I find most helpful?

I couldn't have survived without my family and friends. They supported me when I was down, and helped me by providing activities. My church community was also supportive, and encouraged me to continue my involvement.

A surprising source of support came from fellow widows/widowers, some of whom were strangers. After several years, I became a person who could help others who were newly widowed. Now it seems obvious to me why it was helpful; they are walking the same path as me and experiencing many of the same feelings. Many times it was important to just listen, but sometimes it was important to talk. Both are needed.

Some widows find it helpful to be a part of a grief support group. Others don't feel that they need much in terms of support. Respect their wishes. There is a time and place to share feelings and thoughts, and that needs to be on the timeline of the person who is grieving.

Question: Who am I now?

This was a far bigger issue that I expected. I had lived thirty years as a wife and mother, and all of a sudden Bil was gone and my children were launched. "Who am I? What is my purpose?" In addition, survival questions cropped up: How do I handle the finances? Do I have enough money to support the children and myself?

My identity as a wife was gone. I wasn't part of a couple any more, and I had to relearn how to say things like "meet me at *my* house," instead of "*our* house." A lot of soul searching and experimentation were needed to sort out who I was and who I wanted to be once Bil was gone. Once I did that, I felt like I could make more decisions on my own that fit who I am today.

Another widow asked poignantly, "How long is it going to take to find my new role/purpose?" It feels like forever, and the timeline varies with each individual. Another asked, "When is it okay to be angry?" You never know when an output of emotional energy such as sadness, anger, and sometimes joy, will occur. Let it happen!

Question: How do you support your children or other family members?

Initially I had a difficult time thinking beyond myself, but I reminded myself daily that others also missed Bil. This was especially true for our children, family members, and close friends. Our children had only one parent, and that one was crying all the time! My young adult children created other supports as time passed.

We all found comfort in helping each other talk about Bil/Dad and share memories. There is no way to be both mom and dad, but in conversation, I would bring it up. "I think Dad would say . . ." and that would lead to more in-depth and meaningful discussions. Another widow makes the distinction that she became a solo parent, not a single parent.

I felt that since I was the only surviving parent, I owed it to my children to do my very best to stay healthy. I decided to continue exercising regularly, see the doctor for the little things that are concerns, and try to eat and live well. Through this process, I've maintained a healthy lifestyle that has helped me enjoy my life today.

I also realized that it is not only family that is affected when someone dies. Friends and colleagues also feel a deep loss. Bil's coworkers felt their work environment would never be the same without him, and that is still true nine years later. They had subbed for him when he was sick and supported him emotionally, and now they continue to remember him.

Question: What books did you read?

I read several, but the ones that meant the most to me are here:

Thin Places: Where Faith is Affirmed and Hope Dwells by Mary O'Keefe (Beavers Pond Press. 2005) was very significant for me as I felt that I received messages from Bil many times, and it was wonderful to read about others who had also received messages.

My favorite story is about a cat. Before Bil died, I had suggested that he get a pet, maybe a cat, to keep him company while I was at work. He declined, stating, "You can get a cat when I'm gone." Five days after he died, the family was sitting down for dinner, and a stray cat showed up at the door, insisting that he be let in. He is still with me today, keeping me company, and causing me a few gray hairs!

Another story is related to a home maintenance task I needed to finish. I went to a store to get parts and met with a saleswoman who was also a widow. She understood my predicament! When she went home that day, she opened the local paper, read an article about Bil, remembered that her children had him as a teacher, and realized that I was the one she had worked with that day. I felt that it was Bil who helped me choose her out of all the salespeople in the store, since she would understand and have a connection through the children. When I went to pick up some order, I spent extra time talking with her.

Healing After Loss. Daily Meditations for Working Through Grief by

Martha Whitmore, (1994, 2002) is helpful if you have a short attention span. I had a hard time the first year thinking beyond the next hour or two, so this book was good for me. A short reading for each day offered me plenty to think about, react or relate to, without having to spend time trying to absorb information. The author lost a daughter and describes her own experiences, along with sharing ideas and readings from others.

A Widow's Story: A Memoir by Joyce Carol Oates (HarperCollins Publishers 2011) is a great book full of raw emotions that clearly followed the sequence of events for coping with death in the first year.

Question: Did you journal?

Many people suggest journaling. I wrote occasionally and decided that I would focus my journaling on a specific topic, otherwise I would not do it! I wrote about the messages from beyond and the "thin places" (see Mary O'Keefe's book) that I experienced. Later, I could look back and see how he visited me, and see how I changed and coped with the loss. There were also times when my mind was racing, and I couldn't sleep or think, so I wrote my feelings and thoughts down on paper. I felt calmer and more focused once I had completed my writing.

Question: What about your faith?

Some find church helpful, and their faith in God helps them cope. I found the church community to be supportive and helpful, but since my questions were unanswered and I felt unsupported by God in helping

Bil fight the cancer, I found that church was not working for me after he died. Instead, it was helpful to develop my spirituality in other ways such as reading books, meditation, yoga, and looking for messages/ coincidences in daily activities.

Other widows have found their faith community a source of support and comfort. Even so, they have many unanswerable questions, and feel that God should have the answers. Why did this happen? Bil impacted so many lives. Why him not me? If anyone has answers to these questions, please write a book!

Question: How do I remember him?

I think this is one of the most important questions to answer for yourself. I found it helpful to channel my grief energy into a positive activity that helped me remember him and our values and life together. One thing I did was to write down as many things as I could think of while they were fresh—silly stories, quotes, and memories of activities we did together. (Ask your family and friends for stories to add to the collection.) It was comforting to focus on those memories instead of the dying process.

I tried to complete many of the activities and goals we had set out as a couple, as I knew that would be a good way to remember and honor him. For example, we had started a long-distance bike ride across the country. Since he died, I have continued the ride and hope to complete it sometime in the next few years.

I found it important to choose an activity to remember the person, not the death. I have set up an account through the hospital where Bil received treatment and work jointly with a high school to raise funds for individuals and families coping with cancer. I wanted the fund to focus on the values that were important to us as a couple and as a family. Over the years, we have collectively raised over $50,000. It has helped fund a variety of activities including plane trips to visit family, car rides to look at Christmas lights, celebration dinners, house cleaning, and trips to the zoo. More information can be found at https://bilganglrelay.wordpress.com.

I set up a scholarship for students and another one for teachers. I am amazed every year at how important it is for the individual winner of the award to be linked to Bil and what he represented. There are many others who do volunteer work, plant a tree, or build a bench in a favorite spot.

I continue celebrating Bil's birthday. I encourage other grief travelers to gather your family or do it on your own, tell stories, look at pictures, listen to music-whatever helps you remember him.

A widower mentioned that when he reads about other people doing similar work as his spouse, it helps him to remember and appreciate the talents that she shared with the world.

One widow told me to spend quiet time on the annual death day. I continue to do this every year. I spend that day re-reading sympathy cards, listening to his music, and looking at mementoes.

Question: What do you do when someone says something hurtful?

I reacted sometimes to people that said hurtful or thoughtless things to me, such as "You should be glad you had thirty years." Internally I was saying, *What about the thirty years I won't have?* Nine years later, I can now say I am happy for the thirty years I had, but the pain in that earlier moment clouded that thought.

Another comment is "Time heals all wounds," but a widow friend says, "No, it is scabbed." Or maybe you hear "Time has gone so fast." My response was, "For me, every day is a long day," or "This was the longest year of my life."

Now I say, "Time softens all wounds." We don't heal, we adapt to our new situation. We don't forget, we'll never forget. It gets better, slowly but surely.

Remember that friends and family mean well and are trying to be supportive. I taught myself not to react, but to listen first and find nuggets or ideas that might be helpful to me.

Question: What activities can you do to help yourself?

The list of activities is long. To deal with the grieving, consider counseling or a grief group. I found it most helpful to talk with others in a 1:1 setting about widowhood. Don't put your grieving on hold. If you do, it will whip around and get you later, maybe in the form of depression, excessive drinking, or in other unhealthy ways.

I continued my yoga practice as well as other physical activities, such as swimming and biking. I can't tell you the number of times I found myself crying while I was swimming, or at the end of yoga.

Physical activity helps release pent-up emotions.

Be active and social. Get out and be with others. Live life fully. "Live above the line and visit below the line," another quote of Bil's that I took into my new life as a widow. To me, that means that I should spend most of my time and energy doing activities and being positive, but don't pretend that I don't have down, sad, or angry times.

Question: What tasks should you complete?

I found it helpful to change everything from our name to my name only. Not everyone feels this way, for sure. I did it because it was hard to see mail coming to the house addressed to Bil Gangl. Internally I was screaming, *DON'T YOU KNOW HE IS GONE?* It added to my pain.

You know how hard it is to be the one left behind. Think of your remaining family. Write a will, an advanced care directive, and then write letters to future generations that are audiotaped that include pictures and some history about your childhood or family that would be helpful for future generations. Or make things for grandchildren or children when they get married. Make a video of yourself reading to your future grandchildren. The ideas are endless.

Question: What should I do with his clothes/possessions?

There is no right or wrong answer. I have one friend who got rid of all the clothes right away and sold the house. All the memories associated with those items made it hard to focus on the day in front of her.

185

Another friend has not given away or sold any clothes or possessions. A widower told me that he got rid of everything within the first month. He said, "There was no need for it in the house and it wasn't practical to keep it."

I did it in stages. First, the things that were not personal, then his clothes, then some of his possessions or things he made. My process was to look at the item and listen to my feelings. Did I have a memory of him wearing the shirt? Or making the art? Or using the tool? If I shed a tear, then it wasn't time. You will know when it is okay to get rid of things, just keep asking yourself if today is the day.

Another idea is to give items to others in the family or his friends who will appreciate them. I have been very surprised at people's positive reactions to this, and it is always a reminder to me that many people have meaningful memories of Bil, not just me.

Question: When did you take off your wedding ring?

Do what feels right for you. There is no right or wrong answer to this question. One obvious but not easy answer—take it off when you don't feel married anymore. That doesn't mean you want to remarry. It is when you accept the fact that he isn't coming back and your heart has started to heal. I stopped wearing my wedding ring after eighteen months, then wore it around my neck for another year. Now I wear that necklace when I go to an event that relates to Bil. I feel closer to him when I am wearing it. Other widows remove the ring right away, and others never remove it.

Question: Should I start dating again? If so, when?

This question has many right answers. Some choose to date right away, and others do not want to date again. It varies with age, interest, and opportunity.

Bil encouraged me to love again. I remember saying, "No way. There is no one else but you." But sure enough, it happened. Loving a new person, or even dating, honors the love that you shared with your spouse and gives you an opportunity to share and focus on living today. It shows that you appreciated loving someone, sharing activities with someone, and adds purpose to your life.

I found that I didn't feel comfortable with online dating as many do, but instead joined clubs that allowed me to do activities I loved, such as bicycling, and gave me an opportunity to meet others who also like the same activities. If you decide that you want to date, you need to help make it happen. Make yourself available by being involved in activities and take the initiative to meet new people. The goal doesn't have to be a date, but making a new friend. Who knows where it will lead?

Question: What do you recommend to the griever's friends?

When you send a sympathy card, be sure to include stories or memories you have about the person who died. Those stories are an invaluable link to the person and they honor the relationship. It is heartwarming and reminds the widow that she is not the only one who remembers him.

One widower stated, "I heard praise for my late wife. It confirmed what an incredible person she was, and I learned the impact she had on others. She saved lives."

Invite newly widowed people to social gatherings, with or without a friend. Don't be afraid to say the deceased person's name and tell stories. After Bil died, I did many activities with women. What happened to the men friends from our group of friends? Were they staying away? Or was I not fostering those relationships? I missed their companionship and conversation. Eventually that changed as I became more comfortable with my new life.

Prior to Bil's death people asked us, "What can we do?" We told them that we prioritized time with family and friends, and asked friends to prioritize this for themselves too. We heard from a few families that they took a vacation that they had been putting off.

Many people want to provide meals, but that is not always what is needed. In fact, it may offend someone who feels capable of doing his/her own cooking, and s/he would instead appreciate other things. Make sure you ask what you can do, but offer specifics and follow through. Don't just say you will help—do it!

Continue to support new widows with basic home maintenance. I remember how much help we had when Bil was sick, whether it was with meals, lawn mowing, or snow shoveling. After he died, there was silence. I needed the help more than ever after he died. I was so low, I had the whole house to maintain, and I needed to return to work. One widow friend put it this way: you find out who your real friends are.

In a nutshell, this is what I learned: pay attention to your grief and your feelings at that moment. Try to stay in the present, but plan for the future. Trust yourself and your instincts about how and when to do new activities or work through an issue.

I hope these ideas are helpful to you in your process of grieving after loss. There is not one way, or a right or wrong way, but there is the way that works for you. Keep moving through the process. Peace.

~Megan.

CHAPTER 15

HUNTER
by his mother, Ingrid

David speaks:

I recently joined a writer's group. One of the members told me that she had a friend who lost a son to opioids. She suggested that I contact her friend, Ingrid. I did. Ingrid agreed to write about her grief, the life and loss of her son, Hunter, and describe her journey through the valley of grief.

Ingrid writes:

Our oldest son, Hunter, was the much anticipated, much-loved baby born after the loss of our first daughter, Alexandra, who was stillborn. He "delivered" (pun intended) to expectations with his large, twinkly, brown eyes, gorgeous long lashes and lovely shiny black hair with "cow curls." A cherub-looking baby, he was the culmination of all our parenting dreams. He was joined sixteen months later by Jake, and nine years later to the day, by Cooper. Tom and I, avid downhill skiers, saw our future full of family ski trips with our three children.

Through toddler and elementary school days, Hunter preferred playing with Legos, Hot Wheels, Tonka trucks, G.I. Joes, and pretending to be James Bond 007. He dreamed of going into the Army. Our golden retriever, Charlie, was his constant companion. People asked, "So, you named your dog, Charlie, and your son, Hunter? Didn't you get those names mixed around?"

We read books upon books to him. He spoke early, around eighteen months. I recall easing him from his car seat onto the parking lot of Kohl's department store. He stood in his forest-green bomber jacket with denim sleeves, navy cords, and navy sneakers with white bumpers, and dark soft hair peeking out from a forest-green cap replete with brim, earflaps, and fleece lining. I tightly held his hand. Walking to get her toward the store, he exclaimed, "Look, Mom, my H!" pointing to the capital H in the middle of the enormous storefront KOHL sign. Oh, how wonderful is the world that revolves around you!

Hunter adored his dad, Tom. Once Jake came along, Tom had Hunter with him whenever he was not at work. Hunter delighted in wrestling with Daddy. He squealed with delight when he jumped on his father's crouched back. Those videos I took are now so precious. Hunter would riddle Tom with questions always initiated by addressing his father in triplicate.

"Dad, Dad, Dad, do they pick us, or do we pick them?" Hunter inquires, regarding his ever-present interest in girls.

"Dad, Dad, Dad, did you get hearts in your eyes when you met Mom?" referring to the cartoon he had seen earlier that morning.

Our darling boy grew into a handsome young man. I sometimes

said it was good that he was so aesthetically pleasing because he could be a handful, always clear on what he liked and wanted. He made the best of his good looks and augmented them with an ability to charm people should he so choose. He could use his strength of character, confidence, and persistence to get what he wanted. Sometimes that combination of traits was charming, sometimes intimidating, and most often, persuasive.

Hunter was our down-home boy. You might spot him cruising in his white Tahoe with a ball cap, cool shades with colored reflective lenses, and a big grin. He loved seventies' rock, new country music, and driving through the Wisconsin countryside with his buddies. He could talk you blue in the face about cars and trucks. In the winter, he added downhill skiing to his repertoire of favorite activities. He worked at Afton Alps Ski Area in the ski shop, mounting bindings and tuning skis. Hunter loved skiing and loved skiing fast.

Hunter graduated from high school in 2010 and went to university, not his choice, his parent's choice. Realizing that wasn't his path, he packed up to attend a two-year college in northern Michigan for Ski Area Management. He seemed to enjoy the program but stopped midway through the second semester after yet another knee injury borne from his aggressive skiing. He moved home that spring acting listless and moody. We felt Hunter had so much potential and recommended he focus on one of his passions to build a career.

That summer he worked at a local convenience store. His hours were irregular, and he'd often come home late. Tom and I decided we needed to confront him to get him back on track. It was a Sunday evening, a night when all of the responsibilities and deadlines of the approaching workweek come rushing back. After waiting up for a few hours for Hunter, I resigned myself to get some sleep. Tom said he'd stay up until Hunter came home and talk with him.

The next morning as I woke, Tom came and sat on my side of the bed. "Ingrid, I talked with Hunter last night. He said he has a drug problem and needs help. He wants to go to treatment."

I sighed. I climbed the stairs to Hunter's room and prepared myself for an onslaught of my senses. The room is rectangular with walls painted blue, framed photos of military jets and red curtains that connect with the Air Force theme Hunter chose in his younger years. His room had a gorgeous view of Lake Mallalieu. As the oldest of three kids, we bestowed Hunter with the premier upstairs bedroom. Thank God, he can open the window because this summer his room smelled like an old shoe. There were candy wrappers and chip bags tossed on the floor between the bed and the wall, numerous Buckle jeans, collared Ralph Lauren shirts and all sorts of T-shirts with ski manufacturer logos strewn on the floor that construct a sort of rug on the path to his bathroom. Hunter was lying on his bed, covers messy, hair strewn about. His eyes watered the minute he saw me.

"Hunter," I said, "Dad tells me you asked for help. I want to start by saying how proud I am of you for asking."

"Mom, I've tried to stop on my own. I just can't." His voice was halting, and there was such shame in his expression.

"It's okay, Hunter. We'll get through this," I reassured him. "Tell me, Hunter, what kind of drugs are you using."

I expected him to say pot, maybe cocaine, possibly meth. I wasn't at all prepared when he replied, "Heroin, Mom."

My response wasn't one of my proudest parenting moments. "Heroin, Hunter? That's like New York City, lying-in-the-street kind of drug!"

"Not anymore, Mom."

Thus began my education in opioid addiction.

Hunter first went to treatment on July 4, 2012. Yes, we drove him to treatment on Independence Day. Some irony there perhaps?

All I thought at that point was that I wanted my handsome, confident, promising boy back. I believed that after thirty days in treatment it would all be over because our son was, in my view, more intelligent, savvier, and tougher than other addicted kids. He would surely be more successful than average in his recovery.

Plus he had the benefit of a supportive family and extended family, good insurance, and parents who would pay out of pocket for any other services needed. I believed he would be one of the few that will be "one and done" with treatment.

I recall fiercely thinking that to help him I would leverage all the knowledge and skills I learned from my twenty-five-plus years in the corporate world, including the last fifteen years focused in the healthcare and pharmaceutical industries.

What I didn't understand at this point, first and foremost, is the dreadfully addictive nature of the drug. I didn't even begin to comprehend the lock it had on Hunter's brain. I certainly didn't grasp that it was the interwoven structure of pharmaceutical companies, regulatory agencies, doctors, pharmacies, legislators, and the legal system that have, intentionally or not, built a vast industry that feeds, grows, and defends the use of opioid painkillers.

Hunter went through cycles of treatment, recovery, and relapse. To wean slowly from opioids, he tried methadone on the advice of friends who were seeing success on that path. The prescribed two-year treatment of successively lower and lower doses seemed way too long. He was impatient, and we were impatient. He ramped down too quickly and was in terrible pain for over six months. We were not as empathetic and understanding of his pain and sickness as we could (should) have been. He relapsed. It was 2014, and I was losing hope.

In December of that year, Hunter had completed another round of treatment in Minnesota. The insurance company would only approve ten days of inpatient treatment because he had been in treatment three times prior, was doing well with this treatment, and was committed to his sobriety. I was desperate to find him a safe, structured, supportive place to live. The preferred destination was a step-down program at his current treatment facility. But it was not covered by insurance. We were willing to pay, but at the same time looking for alternatives.

Through my company's employee assistance program, I received a recommendation for a treatment facility in Prescott, Arizona. The significant advantage of this program was that patients were required to stay for a minimum of three months in inpatient treatment before they could go into a step-down program. The kicker for me was that they could remain in the program for up to two years. The center would even help them acquire work or attend the local college.

In early December 2014, I was sitting on the Minneapolis airport tarmac in a jumbo jet for what turned out to be eight hours. I used the time to call the Arizona treatment center, understand their program and to negotiate the price. Before takeoff, I was also able to arrange for my parents to drive Hunter from the current treatment center to the Minneapolis airport to fly to Phoenix. He would be met at baggage claim and escorted to treatment.

This treatment worked well for Hunter. He was in the program for almost two years. He relapsed twice, but on his third stay, he found success and confidence in his sobriety. He became a leader at the center. He was known for his ability to insert his delightfully wicked sense of humor at just the right time to lift the mood in the room, and for cooking amazing mega-meals for twenty people or more.

He called us from treatment in July of 2016. Hunter was twenty-four years old. He shared that he had been admitted and had acquired financial aid to go to school at Wyotech, a well-respected automotive repair school in Laramie, Wyoming. He spoke rapidly about his ideas for the future and the logistics of picking up his beloved truck at our home in Wisconsin and driving it back to school.

Hunter was a phenom at school. His grades were excellent; his class rank ranged from first to third depending on the week. He never missed a day of school. He built relationships with his instructors to assure that he had full comprehension of the material. He went to tutoring each day after school. He attended local AA meetings and acted as an AA sponsor for two local youths. The Arizona treatment center asked him to return over Christmas and speak about his recovery and success at school.

Hunter called Tom and me three to four times each week. We came to expect that around 9:00 p.m. our (Central) time. Hunter called and updated us on his day, the subjects covered in school, and his latest plan for his future. Hunter's objective was to graduate at the top of his class as NASCAR recruits from this select group. Hunter was hell-bent on working for NASCAR.

Our phone calls with Hunter in November included an invitation to come home for the Thanksgiving holiday. He was reticent. He said he was concerned about the unpredictable weather, the possibility that blowing snow might close down the highway into Laramie, which could result in him missing a day of school. However we were relentless, and Hunter acquiesced to coming home.

It was awesome to see him. We finally got to experience Hunter as a mature adult. He was happy, proud, and gracious. He spent the weekend deer hunting with Tom, playing with his seven- and ten-year-old nephews, and talking with our family crew of grandparents, siblings, cousins, aunts, and uncles at the Thanksgiving table. Hunter heaped on his plate his special requests for dinner; homemade spaetzle and German salad both made from the recipes handed down from his great grandmother who was born in Heidelberg, Germany.

I remember hugging him about twenty times that weekend, saying, "I love you. I'm so proud of you."

Hunter apparently relapsed on Sunday. Tom talked with him on the phone Monday morning as Hunter walked to school. We weren't able to get in touch with him after that call. I was to leave for a trip to Europe on Wednesday of that week. The following Monday at 2:00 a.m., two police officers stopped at our house to inform Tom that Hunter had died on Sunday, December 4, 2016, a week after we had put him on the plane back to school.

My cousin Deb, a Lutheran minister, officiated at the funeral. Her gentle touch, deep understanding of Hunter, and sense of calm brought an aura of respect and love to the service. Hunter's ten-year-old cousin did an incredible job of reading a Bible verse. Tom had chosen to include two of Hunter's favorite songs, "Have You Ever Seen the Rain?" by Credence Clearwater Revival and "Spirit in the Sky" by Norman Greenbaum.

In her sermon, Deb touched on the addiction that caused Hunter's death. The capstone of the funeral was the eulogy given by Hunter's best friend, Kyle, our Wisconsin State Champion Wrestler in 2010, that so captured Hunter's spirit.

This was Kyle's eulogy:

For those of you who do not know me, my name is Kyle Crain, and I was one of Hunter's closest friends. It is with great sorrow that I stand before you here today, but instead of dwelling on our sadness and our

198

loss, I would like us all to think about our friend, son, brother, and grandson, and remember all the great memories he has left us.

Hunter was anything but boring. You were always guaranteed to have a good time with Hunter, and you really didn't have a choice on whether you were going with him or not. He would always call you and ask what you were doing, and regardless if you were busy or not he was picking you up. You always knew once you got into Hunter's car, you stuck for at least an hour.

Whether it was driving around for hours listening to class rock until he forced you to go to his parents' house and lose in pool, driving by his land and shining for deer, taking the boat out on Lake Mallalieu, winning concert tickets, going to Perkins at 3:00 a.m., and running Perkins out of hollandaise sauce, or going to McDonald's drive-thru and having to get him an extra order of absolutely everything he wanted in his McFlurry. Ordering for that kid was one of the craziest things I've ever done.

Hunter was stubborn, smart, funny, adventurous, passionate, and proud. He was always so proud of the way he looked, especially when he got to hang out with his Uncle Bob. He loved his Tahoe, his obnoxious belt buckles, his guns, and his knives, because you know he had more than one on him at all times. There was a drawer full of knives at the Blair's house with all of the knives that Hunter had acquired over the years. Hunter was the type of guy that showed up to your house strapped, with a velociraptor-looking knife hooked onto his, as Hunter would say, "gnarly belt," and another Rambo knife strapped onto his leg. This was all in preparation to go to a PG-13 movie. Hunter told Jake one day when he was home that he was going to get his conceal and carry, yah know, just in case he was ever in a bad neighborhood, and Jake said he looked at him and said, "Hunter, you should NOT get your conceal and carry." Hunter just gave him one of his attitude-filled looks.

This probably isn't a surprise to any of you, but Hunter had a rebellious side. According to Facebook, he studied Windsor and Women at the University of River Falls, and he had been stealing cars since he was thirteen. Tom, cover your ears, but every time Tom was out of town, Hunter and I would steal his orange truck, and every time we got home he had to get the tire tracks to line up just right, and the mirrors had to be the right way. There was one time when Ingrid and Tom were out of town. So naturally, Hunter took one of the cars out. When he was just getting home, his grandpa who lives about a block away was out walking the dog and saw someone driving the car home. So Hunter was confronted by Tom, and he denied, denied, denied, and finally broke and said, "Yah know, what BS! I would never have gotten caught if Grandpa hadn't been out walking the dog at 2:00 a.m.!" Nothing was ever Hunter's fault.

Along with many other things, Hunter was loyal. He may have been a jerk to your face, but you always knew that Hunter cared no matter the difference you had. There was a babysitter that Jake said always sucked and would refer to the boys as the Blair Witch children. One day the babysitter was being dumb, so they locked her out of the house and got all the neighborhood kids together, filled up a bunch of squirt guns, and took her down.

No matter what, Hunter always had your back. You could sit and fight with Hunter about anything and then when the fight was over he would look at you and say, "Dude, you need to chill out."

I want to leave you all with this. Hunter was doing great. He had a 4.0 in school, he was at the top of his class, he was sponsoring two people, and he was finally living out the very thought-out plan he had set out for himself. It is incredibly sad that Hunter has left us, and we are all going to miss him so much, but you know Hunter would not want you to sit here and think anything but the best thoughts of him. So go shoot a gun, go skiing, go smoke a Camel menthol, go listen to some Lynyrd Skynyrd, go buy a scratch off, go laugh until your stomach hurts, go do a goddam burnout, go do something Hunter would do today.

I always knew that Hunter, having the disease of addiction, was at risk for overdose and death. The disease of opioid addiction is chronic and was fatal for Hunter as well as for 42,000 other people in the United States that same year (US Department of Health and Human Services, 2019). Still, his death came as a shock. If you know football, it's like being clipped, hit from behind and laid out on the turf.

Hunter's death created a dissonance in my world. There was an ongoing battle in my mind between reality (Hunter is dead) and disbelief (How could Hunter be dead?). At first, there was the physical sensation of being out of my skin. I was unable to think, stand, sit, walk, speak, or sleep. There was no respite.

Within days, I was able to push myself into work mode, removing myself from the reality of his death and attending to the tactical operations like planning the funeral, writing the obituary, choosing photographs, and designing and selecting the weight of the paper for our thank-you notes.

To complete these tasks, I fooled myself into thinking that we were planning his graduation or wedding. I focused all my attention on celebrating Hunter, my wonderful son, who would somehow magically show up at our home. I could maintain that for minutes, sometimes an hour, and then I'd dissolve back into tears.

I operated in the alternate current of disbelief and pain for four months until I effectively dropped. As I began allowing the reality of Hunter's death into my psyche, I became exhausted, physically and emotionally. Mourning my son would often eclipse all other thoughts. I found myself obsessed with Hunter. At age fifty-two, I felt that the best times of my life had passed. I desperately wanted to negotiate a deal, where I would forgo the next fifty years to relive the last twenty-five.

In April of 2017, I took a leave from work. For me, stepping away from the career I loved was the bravest move I have ever made in my life. I considered myself resilient with a track record of working extremely hard, persevering in the face of adversity and challenge, and fully embracing the joy in each part of my life, family, career, and friends. With Hunter's death, I found that parts of my life didn't matter anymore. Everything fell to the wayside except for caring for my boys and husband, honoring Hunter's life, mourning his death, and trying to survive. "It's just so cliché," I incessantly lament to my grief therapist, because this is my new reality.

Our new family of four rallied around each other. We've each taken different paths in dealing with our common loss. Tom is less apt to speak about it except with his closest friend and me. He's been there for friends who have lost children after Hunter died, and I see that as a benevolence borne from experiencing heartbreak. Jake and Cooper grieve their brother's loss and tend to remember his whole person, both good memories and those times where Hunter acted "as a monster," as they would say. They understandably still hold anger, frustration, and hurt. Tom and I are prone to thinking only of Hunter's positive qualities and idealizing a lost future with him in it.

People often ask, "How's your marriage?" They recite alarming (but false) statistics of the probability of divorce after the loss of a child. For Tom and me, Hunter's death wound us more tightly together. We cling to each other, building a cocoon of solace and sanctuary. We are the only two people who genuinely knew Hunter from birth to death and will carry his torch to our grave. Tom can speak of memories of Hunter that instantly bring his whole being to life for me.

I am continually surprised at the impact and longevity of my grief. Earlier today, over two years after Hunter died, while riding in the car with Tom, I felt the familiar pressure on my chest—emblematic of grief. It's as though a massive stone, like those on the shore of Lake Superior, rounded smooth by the relentless waves, sits directly in the middle of my chest. I experience its mass as if it lies on top of me while I am lying flat on the ground and gravity is pulling on it, crushing my heart and sending pain through my back. The tip of the stone pushes on my throat making it difficult to breathe. I now realize that this experience along with panic attacks, night terrors, and what I call "grief attacks" will come unexpectedly.

I have the attention span of a gnat; and reading, which I love, causes me to fall asleep almost instantly. My family often finds me on the living room couch, fortressed by large, soft, navy accent pillows, with my iPad flopped down and me, asleep.

If I don't outright decline the invitation, I leave the social gatherings, which once gave me energy, within thirty minutes. My mind so distracted by thoughts, *Hunter's dead. Hunter's dead.* It's a rare gift to have someone say, "I think of you often," in reference to Hunter's death. Even better is a person who chooses to share a memory of him. Those moments are precious, knowing that Hunter lives in someone else's mind.

I no longer have the belief that there is life after death. I compel myself to deal with the fact that it is highly unlikely that there is eternal life. "What if he is simply dead? I insist. "I've got to deal with that."

Even so, when I journal, I inevitably start with, "Dear Hunter," continuing to write a letter to him. The most I hope for is some spiritual connectedness with all the living and the dead. In contrast,

Tom is confident that when he dies, he will reunite with Hunter. His belief brings both him and me some solace.

We are fortunate to have every conceivable support available to us. I have learned that not all grief travelers have that. Our friends are incredible and have been extraordinarily compassionate. From them, we have received only kindness, comfort, and support. I had worked for over thirty years at a company with excellent benefits including (I discovered) a dedicated grief counselor. My boss and coworkers went out of their way to rally around me after my loss and truly made me feel valued. Counsel from my exceptional grief therapist, compassionate physician, and my former corporate executive coach have each been invaluable.

I also find comfort in any form of exercise. I try to fit in a run, yoga session, or CrossFit at the gym at least three times per week. I know if I can exert myself physically, my reward will be an episodic reprieve from my grief. I sometimes even feel optimistic after a workout.

My passion in life is altering the trajectory of the opioid epidemic that is ravaging our country. I speak up for those with the disease of addiction as they face such stigma, shame, and marginalization. We have taken the money given in Hunter's memory and placed it into a fund to support nonprofits addressing the opioid epidemic. We were honored to have Hunter's story shared in our local newspaper and included as a video in a hospital foundation fundraiser.

One task comes easily to me. It's speaking at conferences, community forums, and schools about Hunter to raise awareness, educate, advocate, and influence others to take action to stop the scourge of opioids.

I feel far from the competent women I once was. I am humbled knowing that my capacity has diminished, yet it has allowed me to identify and focus on what matters to me in a way that I would never have been able before this tragedy.

Rest in Peace, Hunter Blair.

CHAPTER 16

MY GRIEF STORY OF JAN
by Jennifer

David speaks:

My cousin Jan and I both grew up in Bay City, Michigan. I admired Jan for her kindness, fine manners and her beauty. She was comfortable in her own skin, polite, thoughtful, and compassionate. After I joined the Navy, we didn't see each other often enough.

However, Jan found a creative way to reunite "the cousins." Jan's daughter Jennifer will explain.

Jennifer writes:

My story began in the early 1900s, long before I was born. There were four sisters each raising their children in a small city in Michigan. All four sisters gave birth to two children. Their friendship as sisters gave way to the cousins developing sibling-like relationships. David Francis and my mom were two of these cousins. The bond that began as children remained throughout their lives.

All of the cousins graduated from high school; some moved out of the area or joined a branch of the military. Several married their high school sweethearts, uniting their spouses into the family of cousins. As commonly happens, some relationships among the cousins became distant while some grew stronger. David and Linda and my parents were one of the relationships to flourish over the years. Even with the distance between states, there was a kinship and admiration between the two families.

In the mid-eighties, my mom decided it was time to reconnect all of the cousins and their families. She organized a Cousin Campout that began a summer tradition. Each summer a campground was chosen as a mutual meeting point for all the cousins. Several lived in parts of Michigan and others lived out of state. I have so many wonderful memories from the campouts. I considered them the highlight of my summer. I enjoyed seeing all the cousins and learning all about their pasts. Every year as the tradition continued, new activities emerged: potluck night, hikes, games, and campfire stories.

After a decade or so, the Cousin Campouts ended. Life just goes in different directions, I guess.

Thanks to the campouts, I was able to get to know the Francis family more intimately than I would have otherwise.

Before I can tell you about my mom's death, I need to tell you how she lived. My mom loved to be around people. She was involved in various clubs, attended seasonal concerts, and routinely gathered with friends for dinners. She loved to volunteer at the local theatre. She enjoyed talking with people and making new friends. As a school guidance counselor, she helped her students work through social and academic problems. Many days she shared heart-wrenching stories of the students in need. It was obvious how much she connected with her students.

After retirement, she continued providing guidance to first time homeowners in her community. Again, her dedication was outstanding. She held a lot of pride knowing she helped a struggling family move into their first home. The best part of her career experience was she shared them with my dad. Although he was at a different school district, he was also a guidance counselor. The homeowner counseling was a job they shared.

Physically, my mom was very attractive. It was important to her to remain youthful-looking, which was not difficult since she always looked years younger than her actual age. She wore bright colors, which complemented her complexion. She stayed up-to-date with the latest trends and wore her hair in the latest fashion. I'm sharing this to set the stage for what comes as I approach the grieving stage, not to imply a sense of vanity.

Since my mom loved to be around people, her home was built to accommodate gatherings. Her decorating was impeccable. Her last home is decorated in rich reds and blues. At Christmas, her favorite holiday, the house had a touch of Christmas in every room. She was a fabulous cook and superb baker. She spent hours reading cooking magazines, experimenting with new recipes, and sharing her talents. Every holiday she made her famous cut-out cookies. Rolling her cookies thin allowed her to decorate each one with tremendous details.

She took the time to make every celebration, holiday, or get-together extraordinary.

My relationship with my mom was not a typical mother-daughter relationship. We were more than that. We were friends. She was the first person with which I shared my thoughts. We talked to one another every day. We finished each other's sentences. Frequently we got together and found ourselves wearing the same outfits. She was my number-one cheerleader, encouraging me throughout my life. It wasn't out of the ordinary for her to clean my house as a surprise after my long day of work.

I was always grateful for the delicious meals she made for us nearly once a week. She was my therapist, teacher, caregiver, personal chef, and confidant. My family was fortunate to have her help me raise my two boys. She was always there to lend a hand with transportation or picking up a sick kid from school. Whenever and whatever we needed, she was always there. The thought of losing her was terrifying.

In April 2012, everything changed. After open-heart surgery, she wasn't my mom any more. Recovering from the surgery was a daunting experience. She participated in extensive rehabilitation exercises. She changed her diet and lost a great deal of weight. Physically, she looked fabulous. However, when I looked into her eyes, she wasn't there. She didn't seem engaged with our conversations. She simply nodded and responded with a short answer. A withdrawn, unknown stranger replaced her joyful nature.

In the fall following her surgery, I was remodeling my kitchen. This was a time where my mom would have been a help to my decision-making. I took her with me to choose the color of tile. I expected her to engage with me on the choices of color. I came away from the shopping experience feeling confused. She didn't offer any opinion. She didn't have any comments or thoughts on what I showed her. I didn't understand what was happening. Remember, she was the decorating expert. She loved to create new décor. I was hurt, confused, and frustrated.

At the one-year mark, it was apparent that the "old Jan" was not returning. The mom I once had was no longer there. She had little resemblance to the woman who raised me. She looked the same, wore the same types of clothes, continued with some of the same activities. But she was different. This person was not my mom. Her eyes were distant and sunken. She rarely smiled. Her once-meticulous hair looked matted and unbrushed. She continually wore the same clothes. She contributed less and less to conversations due to poor word recall.

She tried to make us her fabulous dinners. Except they weren't so fabulous. She forgot how to make some of the basic dishes she had made for years. At one point, her best friend from childhood asked her to make the famous cut-out cookies for her daughter's wedding shower. That was the one thing the daughter wanted for the shower: Jan's famous cut-out cookies. So she went about making them. They didn't turn out. So my parents contacted a local baker who made them.

Mom was able to take the cookies without the family ever knowing they weren't "made by Jan." I can only imagine how uncomfortable she felt while everyone raved about the cookies. During this phase of her life, she became a fantastic actress. When she was in public or socializing with friends, she fooled them all. She was able to play the necessary roles keeping her decline secret from those outside our immediate family.

My mom was a private person. She did not want us to share her decline with others. Several times friends or relatives confronted me, "How's your mom?" I came up with my typical response: "Well, open-heart surgery definitely can take the wind out of your sails!"

I protected her dignity. My dad was great at it too. Since they were eating dinner out, he ordered for her. This avoided her frustration when unable to come up with the name of what she wanted to order.

While others still saw her as Jan, I was secretly mourning the loss of my real mother. Our shopping experiences were no longer enjoyable. I would call to share my day. Her responses were short and lacked compassion. I asked her to join me on various excursions, anything just to spend time with her. She either brought my dad or turned me down all together. The woman whose loss terrified me was already gone.

Her usual cleaning rituals became more intense. Now she was getting rid of things, many things: dishes, clothes, jewelry, and decorative décor. She was even throwing out valuable items like an iPad, garage door opener, and utensils.

My dad started going through the trash, recovering valuables. Her diamond ring came up missing as well. This was particularly hurtful to my dad. He handled this as best he could. I remember him telling me, "Your mom didn't lose the ring. Whatever this disease is lost her ring."

She organized all the closets, labeling the containers with their contents. Looking back, I believe she was preparing the house for her death. She was cleaning it out for my dad. She was making it easier for him, except we didn't realize it at the time.

When David asked me to share my thoughts on how I have grieved her loss, I pondered this a great deal. How did I deal with the grief? What got me through it? I believe it was my mom.

She helped me prepare for her death while she was living. The values she taught me as a child included cherishing every day you are alive. When my mom reached a milestone birthday, I asked her if it upset her to be turning fifty. Her response stayed with me: "Why would I be sad? I know that I have lived fifty wonderful years! Now I can keep living many more."

While my mom was declining both physically and mentally, it was apparent that her love for life was gone. It was not the way she wanted to live. We are thankful she did not have to decline to the point of needing outside help. She would never have wanted to live that way. She was ready to go.

In 2016, her decline led to a fall, hitting her head on the garage floor. She died several weeks later. Knowing her life was no longer enjoyable, how could I want her to live?

Perhaps I should explain some of my spiritual beliefs at this point. I was not raised within an organized religion. I was raised to treat others as I would want to be treated, respect others, do my best, and be thankful for the life I was given. I went to a Catholic elementary school due to the local public school issues at the time. I was educated on religion, but have many questions challenging the beliefs. At some point, my thoughts may change; but for now, I am comfortable living my life on Earth, following the Golden Rule.

I find death rather perplexing. We all know that someday we will die. We don't know for certain where our spirit goes after death. I guess we will find out once we get there. I remember Linda sharing her story about a butterfly. It was one year since Jon had disappeared. David was out searching for Jon, while Linda sat with her granddaughter. A butterfly joined them and sat on Linda's finger for an extended period. I loved the story, but also listened with some skepticism. It wasn't until my mom died when my skepticism solidified to affirmation regarding the human spirit after death.

How do I know? This is the best part of my story. My mom tells us. Occasionally, we receive messages of her presence. The first one was the best. Remember the diamond ring that was missing? While she was receiving hospice, I asked her to make it reappear. It did. The morning after her death, my dad went looking one more time for her ring. Opening her jewelry drawer, facing straight up was the diamond ring! We had gone through the drawer numerous times frantically looking. But on this day, the day after her death, it was right there.

Another message we received from her was with of all things, feminine panty liners. While she was receiving hospice care at home, I had moved in. I used her bathroom during this time. One day I found a panty liner laying on the bathroom counter. It was not mine. It was not there earlier. Why was it there now? She was bedridden. No one else was using that bathroom. Due to the circumstances of the time, I just threw it away and forgot about it. The second day after my mom's death, my dad woke early. He felt restless and decided it was time to clean her bathroom, the same bathroom I had been using. As he told me the story, he mentioned finding several panty liners appearing on the counter. He assumed they were mine. Upon comparing our stories, there was no explanation for the appearance of the panty liners. I told him it was a sign from Mom.

"Sure," he said, "but why panty liners?"

"Well, Dad, it's the one thing she knew you would notice." He agreed. Another panty liner appeared in a drawer a week later.

While my mom was alive, she always said she never wanted a funeral. She felt her life should be a day of celebration. So that is what we did to honor her. On the day of her celebration, my parents' house was filled with friends and relatives. There were cousins in the hot tub. Others were playing pool or eating munchies. At a given point, just my dad and I were standing in the kitchen sharing a moment of grief with a hug. Just then the back door simply flew open. There was no one there. No wind. Just a flown open door. Again, Mom was letting us know she was with us.

Midsummer after her death, together with my brother's family, we rented a cottage on Lake Huron. This was a beautiful way to grieve together while creating new bonds. Although her presence was missed, we learned how to redistribute the roles she held as our clan elder. My brother and I organized the cooking, which was always my mom's prime responsibility. Our kids learned how to organize games and activities, another task my mom always prepared. That vacation taught us how to move on, create new traditions, and still honor her legacy by making Swedish pancakes! Interestingly, she joined us on this trip as well. Finding a panty liner after a load of laundry, I knew we weren't alone. It was at that moment the song on the radio was by Supertramp, "Give a Little Bit." If you aren't familiar with the song, it talks about a lonely man, *"take his hand, it will be alright."*

Returning home from vacation, my dad walked into his house to find a garage door opener laying on the counter. He assumed his housekeeper left it after cleaning during the vacation. He asked her how she was able to still leave the house with the opener on the counter. She didn't leave the opener. She still had the one given to her: nor does she remember seeing a remote on the counter when she cleaned.

After many months of being a third-wheel, my dad decided he wanted to find someone to spend time with. I helped him create a profile on a dating site. After corresponding with a woman, he made plans to meet for coffee. Immediately after planning his date, one of the cats was spooked and was stalking a stuffed dog. It was as if the cat had never seen the dog before. Come to think of it, my dad could not recall the dog being on that shelf prior. My dad called me to ask if I knew where the dog had been. The last time I saw the dog, it was in the basement. This was also confirmed with my son who had used the shelf to brace his foot the day before. Fast forward one year. My dad's internet stopped working. The problem was solved with the cable company without a resolution. The technician's last suggestion was to find the router's starting point into the house.

This was in the basement inside a custom-made wooden cabinet. It had not been opened in years. Since it had been painted, my dad had to pry it open. Inside was the outlet where the router should have been plugged in, sitting empty. The cord was laying on the bottom of the cabinet. Once he plugged in the cord, he checked to see how easy it was to pull out. Maybe it was loose and had fallen out? No, to unplug it the cord had to be pulled. It was not loose. Incidentally, my dad's use of the internet drove my mom crazy. She was always complaining about him reading on his phone instead of interacting with her.

We frequently find butterflies as well! While vacationing in Florida, we trekked through a park in the Everglades. As my dad was taking a picture of a bird, a butterfly photo bombed his picture. Recently, my dad took me sailing with his new girlfriend. It was my first time meeting her. Throughout our sail, there was a butterfly flying around the mast, even as we traveled far out into the bay.

I still miss my mom, well my original mom. The mom who loved life. The one who was social, passionate, and the life of the party. I miss having gatherings at her house with every detail impeccable. I miss her lemon meringue pie with the perfect sculptured edges. I miss picking up the phone to tell her about my day. I miss having my shopping partner. I'm sure she misses them too.

Reflecting on my grief, I feel lucky. I was able to adapt to her departure. I was able to say goodbye. Unfortunately, she sacrificed a great deal for me to have that opportunity. For that I am thankful. As I move forward, I know I will experience grief again. Since we don't know who or when, I never leave a stone unturned. I don't want to have a relationship lost with things unsaid. I want to share my love and praise with individuals now avoiding any possibility of regret. But then again, I know I can tell my mom I love her every day; her spirit is still with me.

CHAPTER 17

GREG
by his father, Dan

David speaks:

As Jon's soccer coach, not only did I have great players, but I also had many supportive parents like Dan and Sue Seftick, parents of Chris, one of my most productive scorers. Three of my players, including Jon, have died. Four sets of "soccer parents" have suffered a son's death. One of them was Greg Seftick, Chris's older brother.

Dan writes:

My wife Sue and I stood along the sidelines with other parents on a warm evening in early August watching the boys compete in the quarterfinals of the state soccer tournament. Our son Chris and his friend, Jon Francis, were teammates on this U12 "B" team. They had competed well all season, come together as a team, and qualified for the tournament under Coach David Francis, Jon's dad. We got to know David and his wife Linda during the year. It proved to be the beginning of a long friendship that ultimately would be forged in sorrow in the years ahead.

But after that summer, Sue and I did not stay connected with the Francises. It was not because of any deliberate act on our part or a decision they made. Our connection was diminished because of the choices our sons made. Jon switched to track and cross-country while Chris continued to play soccer. There weren't as many opportunities to be together as when our sons were teammates.

Our son moved up a level the next season based on the abilities he developed under Coach Francis. He continued to improve year after year both on the St. Croix Valley soccer team and as a member of the Stillwater High School team.

Chris's older brother Greg loved the sport and worked hard to improve and learn, but it was evident early that our younger son was the one with the God-given talent and natural feel for the game. Greg played hard through his senior year in high school but never made varsity. Stillwater had an excellent squad in 1997 with many talented players and Greg knew he didn't have the ability to play at that level, but he was still disappointed he advanced only as high as junior varsity.

Chris entered the summer of 1998 with the potential to make varsity his junior year in high school. At least that's what I thought. But early that summer he stretched his ACL and his season was over. With him on the sidelines, his opportunity to be scouted by the high school coaches was gone. He slowly recuperated and played some JV that school year.

As senior year approached, Chris announced he was done with soccer. Sue and I were surprised and disappointed. We tried to compromise by encouraging him to skip summer league but try out for varsity. He was unmoved until his brother stepped in. Greg told him he was foolish to quit now. "You have an opportunity to play varsity, and if you don't try you will regret it the rest of your life. I would have given my right arm to play varsity." Chris heard Greg's message, made varsity, and played as a regular as the season progressed. Whether he realized it or not, Chris had found a mentor in his older brother, a source he would tap often in the future.

In a few years it was Greg who was influenced by his brother. Both boys loved to ski and competed on the high school alpine ski team. When Chris went away to college, we all fell in love with Bozeman, Montana, home of Montana State University.

Greg loved the mountains and the opportunities they offered. Chris's interest in backpacking and rock climbing provided Greg with a chance to continue these activities on his frequent trips west—interests planted and nourished through his earlier high adventure Boy Scout trips. The mountains called to Greg. He took a year off between college and medical school to move to Montana and his love for the mountains increased over the next eight years. He often made time to travel west even during four difficult years of medical school in Minnesota and three grueling years of residency in West Virginia. His back-country skiing and rock and ice climbing competence grew. He felt comfortable in the mountains, yet he respected what nature had to offer and knew he was not always in control.

Greg scouted and skied challenging couloirs that tested his ability physically and mentally. He led rock-climbing routes with Chris and friends in the Wind River Range in Wyoming, climbed ice in Hyalite Canyon in Montana, and summited the Grand Teton and Mount Rainier.

Greg was realistic and practical. His motto, "Live to climb another day," indicated he chose his adventures wisely and admitted defeat when appropriate. Perhaps he most regretted his inability to summit Mount Kintla in Glacier National Park. I know of at least three attempts that failed due to weather or route-finding errors. That summit dogged him until the day he died.

The journals Greg kept were filled with technical details of climbs and backpacking adventures. But tucked in among the details were nuggets of reflection and philosophical musings that revealed his character. One of my most treasured quotes from 2005 told me much about my son. He wrote, "It was again nice basking in the happiness and fulfillment that the mountains had provided. I have yet to find any greater joy in life than completing a challenge with physical danger that nature has designed."

Tragedy struck close to home when we learned that Jon Francis had gone missing in July 2006. Our hearts ached for the Francis family as the search for Jon's body stretched out for over a year. We were truly saddened by Jon's death but couldn't understand the full depth of David and Linda's grief because we had not yet experienced the death of a child.

We worried each time the boys ventured into the back country. But

Sue and I were less concerned than usual when Greg announced he'd be meeting his friend Walker to summit the Grand in April 2011. We had never met Walker, but knew him to be a solid guy with a high level of competence in the mountains. We didn't worry. We should have.

A call from Greg that he was safely off the Grand never came on Sunday. Our calls went straight to voicemail. At 9:45 p.m. on Monday, April 18, 2011, a call came from the National Park Service informing us that Greg and Walker were missing. Their cars were still in the parking lot at the trailhead the day after their back-country permit indicated they would be leaving the park.

Our worst fear had been realized. We cried, prayed, and hoped for a positive resolution. A search-and-rescue effort had begun. We were lost. Our first phone call after notifying family was to David Francis. He was calm, reassuring, and helpful. Sue and I were unsure if we should stay home or head for Wyoming. David said directly and definitely, "Dan, you should to go to the park. You and Sue need to be at the search site."

The rangers were supportive and offered hope the first few days of the search. I kept thinking the guys would be found alive. Even after the search switched from rescue to recovery, I held out hope.

Despite the best efforts of the recovery team, no signs of Greg and Walker were found for four days. I was scared, but carried my optimism with me through the week. But more than being scared, I was confused. *Where can they be?* I don't know how many times that question ran through my mind each day.

Finally on Saturday afternoon, I admitted to myself that my son was dead. My prayer changed from wanting Greg and Walker found alive to recovering their bodies. That prayer was answered only four hours later.

Sue and I returned to the Incident Command Center in Grand Teton National Park for the evening debriefing to find search staff waiting for us in the parking lot outside. We were informed that two beacon signals had been picked up that indicated the presence of two bodies buried in the snow. We were stunned, relieved, and confused.

Park ranger Nick Armitage, acting that day as Field Operations chief, had made a final sweep of the canyon with his transceiver in receive mode as the search and rescue team was being shuttled off the mountain by helicopter that day.

When he picked up the two beacon signals, he radioed for the team members still on the mountain to join him at the site. Probing with ten-foot poles produced no results, but the team dug down about five feet through snow, ice, and rock, then probed again and found the shapes of two bodies. Impending darkness dictated the recovery be abandoned until morning.

A small recovery team returned the next morning and the two bodies were located, recovered, and flown off the mountain. Later that day Sue and I, now joined by Chris, met with the coroner. We were informed that Greg and Walker had been buried under thirteen feet of snow by a massive avalanche off the north face of the Nez Perce. They were found in their tents in a sleeping position.

They never knew what hit them.

My heart was breaking because my son was dead.

As the weeks passed, I came to realize the depth of the pain felt by the Francises and other parents grieving the death of a child. Though it took only one week to find and recover Greg and Walker's bodies, a much shorter time than for Jon Francis, it seemed to take forever.

I couldn't imagine the pain David and Linda felt during the time Jon was missing. Our search was coordinated and conducted by experts. They had to organize their own.

The week following the recovery of Greg's body was filled with planning and preparation. Since Greg had no permanent connections to other people or places, Sue and I felt it appropriate to follow the traditions of our faiths and have a funeral in church here in Minnesota. Greg's body was flown home from Wyoming.

The rituals associated with death and funerals directed my thoughts and actions. Family and friends from all parts of the country contacted us or attended the funeral. We felt the respect and admiration Greg had shared with his family and friends and felt supported in our pain as we grieved with so many others.

But soon we were alone. Others returned to their normal lives, to their homes, families, and jobs. Our lives had changed. There was now a huge void where once a close, intimate relationship had resided. The hole can never be filled, that relationship never recovered. We were in uncharted territory looking for our new normal.

The death seemed even more significant to me because Greg was a doctor. Not only had my son died, but society lost a caring soul, an Emergency Room doctor who wanted to help others. It seemed such a waste he only used the medical skills he had learned and developed for nine months.

I experienced all the different aspects of grief: anger, denial, sadness, loneliness, and isolation. Sue went through her own emotional journey of grief. But we found that while we had suffered the same loss, we did not grieve the same way. Sue is much more private in her grief. I am very public in mine. Through support groups and counseling, we learned that it's okay to grieve differently. We needed each other's support to survive, but could not grieve for our spouse or dictate how they should grieve. Each of us would travel our own individual path.

We were told that a majority of parents that suffer the loss of a child separate. Sue and I both agreed that while we would grieve in our own ways, we could not imagine making this journey without each other's support. She has been a great support to me in so many ways. I expected she would, and she came through. But I also expected support from family and friends, and did not receive as much as I needed.

All I hoped for was a phone call or visit that focused on Greg. I wanted to know others thought about him and missed him. The occasional supportive note or email sharing a story about my son got me through the day.

Sue encouraged me to ask for support, but it seemed, if requested, it would not have the same effect. I had a very difficult time dealing with the loneliness I felt from the lack of sympathy.

I found myself comparing others' support networks to my own and I felt the lacking. Looking back, I felt I had been caring and present to others in their time of need for the most part. Two questions haunted me: why was Greg dead? And why was I so abandoned in my grief?

After several months, I found that the best way to deal with my loss and sadness was to go back to my volunteer activities. Giving of myself and showing compassion lifted me out of my self-pity. Initially it was difficult to be a listening presence without wanting to share my grief. I discovered there were appropriate times to talk about Greg's death and my grief as a means of validating my compassion. I began to sense when another on their grief journey benefitted from knowing I was traveling my own.

Some people even questioned the wisdom of putting myself out there when I was so vulnerable. They asked me how I could do it. My response was, "How could I not!"

Supporting others in need has helped me deal with my melancholy and brought me back among the living. I was certain Greg did not want me to stop living just because he had died.

It also became important to me to record my emotional account of the search and recovery and my memories of my son soon after the funeral, after I was left alone with my sorrow. I started writing about the search-and-recovery week, especially attempting to document the details of events as we experienced them during those difficult, emotional days.

In addition, I made a list of many memories from my son's life:

happy, sad, and some very private ones. I didn't know it at the time, but these personal ramblings would create a permanent description of Greg's unique character and a record of his many accomplishments.

The writing did not occur in any orderly or scheduled fashion. I wrote when I found time and had the inclination. I am not a prolific writer, the kind who can sit at a keyboard for hours and bang out thousands of words. Writing a thousand words or for a couple hours made a productive day. Some days I didn't write at all. In fact, I took six months off during the first anniversary of Greg's death. But writing was effective. It created an outlet for my sadness, gave me purpose, and helped me gain a greater respect for the person that Greg was becoming. He had been growing, learning, and maturing, but I hadn't recognized that about him until after he died and I started writing. This was the greatest gift I received from my effort.

As the memories, pages, and words piled up, I considered more seriously what the writing would produce. While it was serving as a useful outlet for my grief, it seemed it could serve other purposes. Family and friends inquired if Greg's story could become a book. Discussions with published authors indicated such a possibility. David and I met for lunch and I asked him if he thought there was a book in my project. He talked about purpose. Two came to mind immediately: I wanted people who knew Greg to get to know him better and never forget him, and I wanted people who didn't know Greg to read his story and wish they had. David encouraged me to create a book in my son's memory.

After many months, much rewriting, and recurring doubts and soul searching, the manuscript reached a point where my efforts produced minimal improvements. I had reached a point where my skills and effort were maxed out. This frustrated me and made me wonder if I had wasted my time. However, when I compared my current emotional state with those initial days in 2011, I realized this project had brought me a long way on my grief journey. Writing about Greg slowly turned my constant sorrow into an immense respect for him and turned my anger into an appreciation for the years we had together.

We settled on a publisher and a process for releasing our book, *Real Mountains*, in early 2016. Then the project transformed from a labor of love into just plain labor.

The doubts crept back in. Would anybody want to read this first-time author's tribute? In my mind, the success of the book as measured by sales vacillated between it becoming a best seller to not selling a single copy. But that wasn't the purpose behind it. I realized that the book was already a success because it had moved me along my grief journey and would memorialize Greg. The work continued aided by a committed editor, meticulous proofreaders, a talented designer, and a compassionate project manager.

Holding the first copy of *Real Mountains* in my hand made me feel as if I had given birth. Our aim was to create a high quality tribute to Greg. Everyone involved felt we had. There was a great deal of interest initially and many family and friends requested copies. But after the first year, interest waned. We had picked the low-hanging fruit.

I was again frustrated and questioned whether all the time and money was worth the effort. My uncertainty is removed when readers tell me that the book had meaning for them, comforted them in their grief, inspired them, or encouraged them to become more like Greg.

The writing of *Real Mountains* and the effort to share Greg's story has been a seven-year project so far. Interspersed in that time have been rituals, regularly repeating memorials to my son that help me in my grief at the time of their enactment and also in their anticipation.

I made a commitment and shared it with Sue and park staff immediately after Greg's body was recovered. I knew I had to return to Grand Teton National Park and attempt to reach the site of Greg and Walker's camp to stand on the place they died.

Sue, Chris, and I hiked to Garnet Canyon in August 2011 and were led to the campsite by park rangers involved in the search. We have returned to the park every summer since, always accompanied by family or friends. These eight visits-and-counting include five to the Sacred Ground, the place where Greg and Walker died.

I feel closer to Greg in Garnet Canyon than anywhere else. His spirit definitely resides there. But after the fourth visit, something changed. At the Sacred Ground in 2014, I told Greg I had accomplished what I set out to do. I told him I would not return (though I did in 2016). My limbs were less flexible, which made crossing the boulder field difficult. I was at peace.

Our visits to the park continue, no longer only as mourners on their grief journey, but now as volunteers.

Walker and Greg's bodies were recovered at 11:00 a.m. on April 24, 2011. We watched a helicopter rise out of Garnet Canyon, the fixed length line suspended and attached to the sling carrying the body bags. Each month at the same time, I sit on the ski lift chair in our yard and face west, visualizing a helicopter rising among the mountains, bringing Greg back to me. This personal ritual allows me to reflect on Greg's life and our relationship. These fifteen-minute sessions have made me more compassionate with others, more understanding of their life situation.

Our more public ritual is our annual Greg's Night of Light. At sunset on every April 16, the night Greg and Walker died in the avalanche, our family, friends, and strangers are invited to light candles as a symbol that Greg's light continues to shine in our world. This acknowledges that Greg influenced our lives and continues to live on in us because of the new persons we have become from knowing him.

Candles have been lit on all seven continents. On the seventh anniversary, April 16, 2018, I felt myself for the first time celebrating Greg's life on his Night of Light rather than only mourning his death. This is progress!

It isn't necessary to write a book to advance on your grief path. Use any creative skill you possess to produce a memorial to your loved one, channeling your sorrow into a meaningful activity that provides purpose to your day. Paint a picture, carve a statue, make a quilt. Focus on your talent and your loved one as your journey moves forward toward acceptance. Grief is not an event. It is a process.

Sorrow is inevitable if we have been given the gift of someone to love in our life. Sometimes I wish I didn't have to grieve. But how empty my life would have been without Greg in it!

Count your blessings if you, as I, have many to love and who love you in return. Our journeys continue, not on an even footing, but through the valleys and over the hills.

It isn't necessary to be family or longtime friends to be a compassionate supporter to others in sorrow. As we travel the path, sometimes forward, sometimes back, we will meet and find new fellow travelers to walk with us and to share a helping hand or an understanding smile or word along the way.

CHAPTER 18

JOHN
by Coralie Hunter

David writes:

John Hunter was one of my best friends ever. I had deep affection and admiration for him. I most admired his integrity, discipline, and competence (among his many other good qualities). He was the kind of friend you'd want to have whenever you face a difficult decision or a tough challenge.

Having John as a close friend and ally was a double blessing because our families were close as well and I had the chance to work with him. When I was the leader of a men's retreat weekend, I asked John to be my assistant. He performed flawlessly and carried much of the emotional and administrative burden.

When I ran for the Minnesota State Senate, I asked John to be my treasurer, the hardest job on the campaign staff. Again he was superb, and he kept me out of financial trouble. Unfortunately I learned after the campaign that I had frustrated him with my undisciplined spending habits. Fortunately, our long friendship survived. I frequently thought,

I am blessed with such a talented and faithful friend.

John and Coralie drove Linda and me to the cemetery for our son Jon's interment. I sat in the back seat of their car cradling our son's remains.

When Coralie shared the news with me that John had melanoma, I was devastated. *No! This should not be happening!* I was mourning the death of my son, and now my best friend was struggling against cancer.

John and Coralie were determined and resilient in their battle against "the dragon." They fought hard and sought traditional as well as experimental treatments. But John died on March 11, 2011.

Coralie writes:

I lost my husband of almost forty-eight years to what I called "the dragon." The correct term is melanoma cancer.

I was born and raised in a small farming community in Northeastern Colorado near the Nebraska border. I was an only child, which left me without sibling companionship. At age seventeen, in the fall of 1960, I left home to attend Colorado State University (CSU) in Fort Collins. In those days, many women went to college to get their "Mrs." Degree, and I was one of them. CSU offered promise in that endeavor because the ratio of men to women was almost four to one. And I wasn't disappointed. I met my future husband, John Hunter; and, as an added bonus, he was from Denver. *Whew!* My life wouldn't be lived out in a small town.

For our first date, John invited me to a symphony concert and we discovered we both loved classical music. I was a music major, and we nurtured our love of classical music throughout our married life.

Upon graduation, we moved to Minneapolis where John was sent, courtesy of the Air Force, to earn a master's degree at the University of Minnesota's School of Public Health. We discovered the amazing amount of cultural opportunities available in the Twin Cities: theater, symphony concerts, lectures, etc. So after a seven-year stint in the Air Force in many parts of the country, we decided to return to the Twin Cities where John worked at 3M.

By then we had two dogs and seven-year-old twins, Samuel (Sam) and Karlene. We settled in White Bear Lake and eventually found a church we liked, St. Michael and All Angels in Oakdale, where we met Linda and David Francis. We became good friends, almost like family. When our daughter Laura was born, Linda and David agreed to be her godparents. Years later, they welcomed their son Jonathan into their family, and we became his godparents.

The Francis and Hunter families remained connected, cherishing each other's friendship through the years. Together we walked through some very dark hours with them as we all grieved the loss of Jonathan. We too struggled with the death of this amazing person who had so much to give to this weary world. As John and I faced our trial with the "dragon," David and Linda were a steadfast anchor as we rode the roller coaster of living with cancer and the finality of death.

In his late sixties, John had generally been in good health. He was always a disciplined person including eating healthy meals and exercising regularly. The myth present in our minds was that, given his healthy lifestyle, he was impervious to contracting a chronic incurable disease. When we received the diagnosis of Stage 3 melanoma, we were in shock.

We were certain that in the United States in 2009 there must be treatments to cure this dreaded disease, though one doctor told us that there had not been any medical advances in this area in the last twenty years. And that opinion was confirmed by a second doctor.

With heavy hearts we moved forward trying to mitigate this disease as best we could. That meant surgery to remove seventeen lymph nodes, which would later profoundly and negatively affect his daily activities.

As people of faith, we asked countless people throughout the world to pray for John. One promising answer to prayer came in the form of a potential treatment which was in the clinical study phase. We grasped at it! It seemed so promising because there were minimal side effects. *Yeah!* Life could go on without this annoying interruption. However, shortly thereafter, the cancer "dragon" returned.

At that point, we had to turn to chemotherapy. The side effects of chemo can be immense. As his disease continued to persist, those side effects robbed John of his ability to drive and to continue his fitness program, which in the past we believed would guarantee John a long, healthy life.

Looking back on the process of trying to tame the "dragon," the body becomes almost an enemy. John kept valiantly fighting and often

I was the "drill instructor" or so he named me. Toward the end, he commented, "I'm not afraid to die." That statement shocked me but in retrospect I see that his body was an enemy and wanted free from it.

On March 11, 2011, John left this world for that place we call "heaven," a place we sing about, recite in our Christian Creed and at some level believe in. Then my doubts came. Is there really such a place? How can one be sure? Many people claim that they have been to heaven and back. But I'm not sure I believe them.

Once again, Linda and David were there for me as I struggled to walk through this desolate valley. Linda gave me a book, *Healing After Loss*. It was of immeasurable help. They both checked in with me regularly, especially when holidays were looming.

We frequently spent holidays together, as a family or as a foursome; especially the Fourth of July found us together, cooking out, watching fireworks, sharing life's events together while the children played. No doubt our children wondered, "What could possibly be so interesting to talk about?"

Shortly after John's death, I remember going to church alone and feeling like I only had one side to myself because John wasn't sitting next to me. Attending Minnesota Orchestra concerts was something we had done for years. That didn't remotely seem possible, as I couldn't imagine going alone.

Fortunately, our good friends, Bob and Julie Paschke, with whom we had regularly attended concerts together, called me and said, "We are going to make plans to purchase a subscription to the Orchestra next year. Let's go out to dinner and select concerts we want to attend."

What a wonderful gift they gave me! Going out as a threesome, not as two couples, felt foreign, however, I was able to push myself to go. In doing that, I took one small step toward building a life without John.

Eating dinner alone was also a challenge. At dinner alone, I listened to several of the requiem masses in my CD collection. One I clung to the most was Johannes Brahms *Ein Deutsches Requiem*. Brahms view of death was less fearful and indeed much more comforting than many of the other Requiem Masses.

As the beautiful melodies and harmonies flooded over me, I sensed a level of comfort that I can only call a blessing. Another amazing gift that was of immeasurable help came through the Fairview Hospice Program. This program offers one year of free grief counseling and other programs to help heal those left behind. I took advantage of that, and slowly saw my life moving step by step forward.

I am still living alone and realize that I have accomplished the adjustment. There are many times I think of John, miss his presence, focus on our good times together, and try to forgive myself for all the times that I was not my best self in the relationship.

I continue to be immensely grateful for the strength that God freely gives to those who seek and mourn, for my longtime comforting friendships, and for my new friendships that give me hope and strength for the future.

CHAPTER 19

CHRIS
by his mother, Jan

David writes:

Before Jon went missing, I paid little attention to missing persons' cases. Bad things happen to other people. Not me. I don't remember the time when Chris Jenkins disappeared. But Chris's mother Jan was aware that our son had disappeared, and she called me. Linda and I met Jan and her husband Steve for dinner. We were all members of "the club." We were in a safe place where we could talk honestly and openly about our grief journeys. I immediately thought of Jan when I decided to ask others to contribute to my book.

"Perhaps the greatest triumphs glow in the love shared and self-respect gained while seeking truth and justice. What matters now is what we do about all we've learned and who we have become because of it." —*Footprints of Courage* by Jan Jenkins.

Jan writes:

This is a true story of love conquering fear. It's a story of those who loved Chris Jenkins including many who never met him. By facing adversity with courage, we forged precious bonds—a testament to the strength of the human spirit.

November 1, 2002, started as one of those fabulous Fridays. About to sit down for a shrimp dinner, I suggested to my husband Steve, "Why don't you call Chris (our son in college) and check to make sure he paid his car insurance. Let me speak with him before you hang up."

Shortly after, I heard only silence in the family room. Walking a few steps so I could see Steve from the kitchen, I said, "You didn't let me talk to Chris."

With an anxious and confused look on his face, Steve responded in a strained voice, "Chris is missing."

"What do you mean he's *missing*?" Silence. "So, what's the plan?" I blurted out.

Chris's roommate Ben said that several of Chris's friends had already been contacted, and many people were looking for him. The Halloween costume Chris wore the night before was not in his room, and no one had seen him. We all knew he wouldn't *choose* to disappear.

Sheer panic raced through my body. I knew Chris was in trouble. Little did I know that November 1, 2002, marked the beginning of a journey that would last the rest of my life.

Chris soon became everyone's child. The public craved details, as evidenced by more than 100,000 hits on his website in the first three days.

Motivated by missing person posters in the Twin Cities, people left messages of hope for his safe return. Strangers captivated by Chris's story shared insightful and supportive messages. Here is one poignant example: "Just a stranger: I don't know Chris but his absence is noted in my everyday life: Every trip downtown I'm surrounded by his face. It follows me on my way home, at least an hour from the Cities, where I see the poster on car windows during the commute and then in the parking lot of where I work. Going to a concert on Nov. 2, I kept looking at the faces in the crowd, the blonds with the short haircuts, I imagine to be his face in the corner of my eye . . .We're all watching, looking, and praying."

After four months of uncertainty and agony, Chris's body showed up in the Mississippi River between downtown Minneapolis and Chris's residence. No evidence was gathered. The manner of death on his death certificate was initially listed as "undetermined," and the cause of death was "drowning."

Four years later, on November 17, 2006, we received a public apology from the Minneapolis police chief, Tim Dolan. We felt betrayed by law enforcement since a proper investigation was never done. A social worker overheard a man in prison for other murders bragging about what he and his gang did to Chris. Yet to this day, we don't know what really happened that fateful night. It's a mystery.

One thing is painfully clear: Sixteen years after he disappeared, Chris's father Steve, his sister Sara, and I live with holes in our hearts. Nothing can replace Chris or mend our broken hearts. Thanksgiving, Christmas, his birthday, Easter, etc., there's an empty chair at the table. Chris will always be missing.

"What you leave behind is not what is engraved in stone monuments, but what is woven into the lives of others." —Pericles

In the fall of 2002, Chris Jenkins was on the top of his game as a senior honor student at the Carlson School of Management at the University of Minnesota (UMN). He was also the goalie and co-captain of the UMN Gopher lacrosse team. As his parents, we were understandably proud of Chris's achievements in academics and athletics. But we were most proud of who he was.

Chris was a dynamic leader that his friends counted on, respected, and loved. He offered compassion and support to others at any time. Hundreds of people have told us that Chris loved life more than anyone they had ever met. He lived fully, savoring even routine experiences and making everything an adventure. His positive energy and infectious smile lifted others who knew him. His silly antics easily captivated an audience, while his genuine goodness kept people by his side.

Chris' huge heart started early in his life. His kindergarten teacher told us he was often the first to run to her desk, asking to help his wheelchair-using classmate Jimmy. Though Jimmy had difficulty talking, he and Chris understood each other. At a young age, Chris had already mastered the art of making people feel good about who they were.

A few months after Chris disappeared, his friend Neil Lorntson compiled a notebook with pictures titled, "A Once-in-a-Lifetime Friend." He described Chris as energetic, caring, confident, fun-loving, and extremely generous.

Neil and Chris had played together on many Eden Prairie, Minnesota football teams. Neil wrote: "When Chris told me he was going to try out as an offensive lineman his senior year, I just couldn't picture it. He's not the biggest guy, weighing about 190. Most offensive linemen for Eden Prairie were 250–275 pounds. It's not that I didn't believe in Chris, I just wondered if he could really make up for almost 100 pounds with his heart and dedication. Boy, was I wrong. Chris proved he was tough enough to do it by pushing around guys twice his size all season long. He worked hard, played smart, and just competed with more heart than the guys he played against."

When Neil had surgery and missed his entire senior year of baseball, Chris showed up at his house nearly every day that Neil couldn't walk. Neil says, "Chris sacrificed many of the last times he had in high school because he knew how bad I felt."

"Chris (Jenkins) was an outstanding student in the Carlson School of Management and a talented athlete. Chris exemplifies the educational values of scholarship, leadership, and involvement with others. I have no doubt Chris would have gone on to be a shining star in his professional life, and a continuing source of pride and pleasure to his family and friends. His death is a wrenching loss to the entire university community and to society." —Dr. Robert Bruininks, president, University of Minnesota.

Several of Chris's friends got together to craft one of the eulogies at his Memorial Service. Christian Bailey delivered it flawlessly:

"No matter how you knew him—Chris, Christopher, Jenks, or Schmenkins—he always left you feeling like you mattered. He had the ability to melt your insecurities away and make you feel welcome. He lived passionately, confident but never cocky. Chris stood up for what he believed in; most importantly—his family and friends. He never lived his life for other people; but he always included everyone in his life . . . Jenks exemplified all that is right in this world: he took the path less traveled. Quick to make you laugh, genuine even in jest, Jenks, we mourn our loss with heavy hearts. We will celebrate the gifts you have given us so generously. It was an honor to have known you and a blessing to be your friend. We are going to miss you, Jenks, but we will never, ever forget."

We survived four months of looking for Chris and years of seeking justice. We prayed, constantly. Steve and I even asked God to take us instead of Chris. We felt we had already enjoyed a full life. Our faith, along with the continuous support from family, friends, and strangers sustained us through gut-wrenching days and sleepless nights.

We struggled to understand that unanswerable question, "Why?" After Chris's body surfaced in the Mississippi River, our faith became a roller coaster. It challenged us for years as we tried to comprehend why God allowed our remarkable son to die at the hands of evil in the prime of his life. Chris had so much more to give.

We have reached out and helped others. Tragically, hundreds of young men have disappeared in the past twenty years under very similar and suspicious circumstances. Because we pushed law enforcement to do something and appeared on numerous national and local newscasts, many parents of these young men contacted us for advice and support. The most difficult aspect of assisting others means that we relive our own loss and grief. It has prolonged our healing process. Yet how could we not help these grieving parents?

We have been there and know how critical support is to parents who suffer from the unresolved death of their child. As of this writing, Chris's case remains the only one of these unsolved cases that has been changed to homicide.

I've spoken to more than 20,000 people (students and adults) about the dangers that lurk in our midst. I believe my "Got Your Back" keynote talk and my book, *Footprints of Courage*, have saved lives. Many students have contacted me through texts, Facebook, emails, and written notes to tell me what my outreach has done to save a life.

Experts helped us. We did everything humanly possible to seek the counsel of professionals to verify what we had learned about Chris's death and autopsy. Butch Hendrick and Andrea Zaferes of Team Lifeguard Systems, Inc, global leaders in water rescue and recovery; Dr. Michael Baden, chief forensic pathologist for the New York State Police; and Dr. Cyril Wecht, forensic pathologist and consultant in many high-profile cases are among those who looked at Chris's case and his autopsy. Their conclusion was unanimous "beyond the shadow of a doubt, Chris was murdered."

We learned that we belong to a club no one wants to join, yet it demands the highest price: losing a child. Many believe that pain is at the very edge of what human beings can bear.

Eventually, we accepted the fact that the life we knew was gone forever. We needed to create a new life and fully grasp that Chris was never coming home.

The most frequently asked questions we have heard are, "How did you stay so strong? How did you keep going?" Here is what I wrote in response:

Our compelling drive, rooted in enduring love for Chris, stayed strong as a result of our unwavering *belief* in Chris; a rock-solid *purpose*: find Chris, seek justice; acting with *courage* regardless of circumstances; a *commitment* to stay the course; and *resilience* to keep going, in spite of setbacks. (from *Footprints of Courage*)

In my desire to help others, I created a model from these principles that I use in my leadership development coaching and consulting:

Courage Edge™

Finding a way forward and leading through uncertainty.

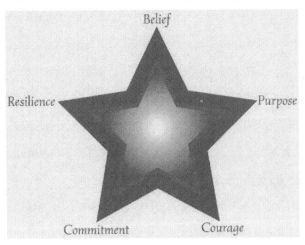

Steve Jenkins offers a father's perspective:

"We have learned to live our lives without Chris. We can't change what happened. All we can do is love each other more. The anger and frustration of dealing with law enforcement made our loss so much harder to bear. We were so naïve about how law enforcement really works. Sadly, they blocked many of our efforts.

Yet I'm stronger because of our unflagging determination and persistence in seeking the truth about what happened to our son. Chris was worth fighting for.

I'm more sensitive to others' pain: their deep sorrow, utter terror, and extreme anxiety. The awareness of evil and horrors of murder are so real to me now; I truly get how fragile life is. I see how life could have been different and I'm sorry it's not how we thought things would be. I've come to learn how to live with a hole in my heart; I miss my son and love him to the nth degree. I think of Chris every single day and can now smile and laugh at his memories.

At the same time, I still cry occasionally, especially when I watch movies. Every movie reminds me of the life that was stolen from Chris and us. Committed to living the best life I can has helped me understand the value of hope. I believe in a future that includes being reunited with Chris."

Steve's commitment as a father continued, demonstrating deep and enduring love, long after his adored son disappeared.

Early in 2008, Steve received the following email:

Mr. Jenkins

Let me tell you one more time how incredible you have been in the last 5 ½ years. Chris and I often joked about you and my dad coaching us when we were pip-squeaks.

Your coaching never stopped. You have lived by faith and in doing so have brought more positive out of such a terrible time than anyone could have ever imagined.

From a friend of your son's I appreciate all that you have done, and as a man I stand in awe of you and your strengths.

Thanks for being such a great example of what a father and a man should be.

Todd Downing

Sara Jenkins Lightner offers a sister's perspective: "Never leaving one of our own behind may not have been the easy path; but for us it was the only path."

At the age of twenty-four, Sara was forced to come to grips with evil in the world. Innocence left in a heartbeat. She supported Steve and my efforts to find the truth and was often at our side as we stumbled forward. We can't make things better for Chris or for Sara. That's harsh for a parent. Similar to Steve and me, Sara carries the heavy weight of learning to accept the utter finality of Chris's life on earth as a member of our family. She struggles with the reality of creating a new identity. At one point she said, "I don't know who I am. I'm not even a sister anymore."

Siblings can lose their parents, to some degree, especially in the early years when parents are overwhelmed with their own grief. People continue to ask us, "How are you doing?"

People also ask Sara, "How are your parents?'

Sara could likely count on two hands the number of people who have asked her, "How are *you* doing?" We know that our daughter Sara needs our love and attention. She was robbed of her only sibling. I hurt for the pain I see in her eyes and heart.

The excruciating pain of missing and murder is still very real for all three of us. While it changes with time and effort, no one gets over the hell of missing and murder. Murder is the ultimate crime where so many lose.

Sara loved her brother deeply. Though Chris was a college student in Minnesota, and Sara worked in Cincinnati, they spoke often to each other. They both enjoyed their new adult relationship established about a year before Chris disappeared. Sara bought a complete stereo system for Chris's car when he was a college senior. Chris climbed out his bedroom window onto the roof, literally shouting from the rooftop, "My sister Sara is the best sister in the whole world."

When I wrote *Footprints of Courage*, I consulted with many people about Chris, especially Sara. I wanted many voices in the book because Chris had such a huge network of people. Chris brought laughter and love to Sara's life, especially in tense moments. During one of my conversations, Sara shared the agony of planning her wedding. For years she had talked about the excitement of watching her brother walk down the aisle on the arm of one of her friends. Now her deep desire to share the joy of her wedding day with her brother—will not be fulfilled.

Sara said, "The excitement of getting engaged was bittersweet in my world. This event marked the first of many life-changing events Chris would not be a part of, now or ever. Just the thought of planning a wedding my brother could not attend actually made me physically ill. I vividly recall driving and crying to the point of throwing up, whenever simple wedding details crept into my mind. I remember just before we walked down the aisle, Dad sewed Chris's ring to my bouquet. Any time my finger touched his ring, I felt stinging tears. Throughout the ceremony I stared at a huge cross bearing Jesus which hung on the wall behind the altar. 'Dear Jesus, please help me.' What I wanted most on my wedding day was to hold it together."

Sara's sadness is palpable. She aches for the joy her children, Cayman and Jace, have missed because they never had a chance to meet their Uncle Chris. The laughter, fun, excitement, and anticipation of "Uncle Chris is coming over" will never be.

As Sara says, "Chris loved children. He would have been a personal playground for Cayman and Jace."

Sara arrived at two profound realizations: 1) If Chris knew he would save dozens, maybe hundreds of lives by losing his own, he would have submitted to God's will; and 2) as hard as he fought for his life, now we must fight for ours. To honor ourselves, and the remarkable life Chris led, we needed to create a life worth living.

When I'm struggling and talk to Sara about my anxiety she often

says, "Mom, you've been through much worse and come out okay."
After all these years, Sara concludes, "The pain never goes away. You
just learn how to live and cope with it differently."

Jan gives a mother's perspective: "When you love someone with all
your heart, their death claims the sacred part of you tightly connected
to them. The moment we heard Chris was missing, our lives changed
forever. We had been thrown into foreign waters. We felt lost. During
all those weeks we spent looking for Chris and then seeking justice, I
couldn't find my way around Minneapolis.

I no longer drove in that city because I had lost my way. *Chris, we
miss you beyond measure!* A part of me is gone—it's with Chris—a part
of me died with him. The stark reality of "no more" is still hard to bear.
No more hugs, laughs, joy of celebrations together. Chris lost his
future, and we lost our futures too."

Rebuilding takes strength, courage, and accepting what is. Steve,
Sara, and I had the monumental task of figuring out how to live a new
life without Chris. Many questions plagued us: Who am I? Why am I
here? Where do we go from here? What is heaven like? We have all
said that we have a heightened awareness and compassion for others'
trials, pain, and heartache.

People often tell us they don't know what to say to those who have
experienced profound loss. I respond, "Just say, I'm so sorry." That's so
much better than all the trite phrases we've heard, which hurt even
though we know they are being said with sincerity.

Life is fragile. I finally understand the impact of that reality.

I cherish every moment, consciously focusing on gratitude throughout the day. I don't have the life I want, yet this is the life I was given. Chris would want all of us to live fully. To honor ourselves and him, we find the bright spots in life and create as much happiness as we can. This is a journey and we certainly have not "arrived."

As Margaret Lee Runbeck said, "Happiness is not a state to arrive at, but a manner of traveling."

We've gained a close friendship with many of Chris's friends. What a rich blessing! They walked at our side for many months; some years. I'm convinced that the strongest bonds between human beings are forged in facing adversity together. Some of the best things in our lives rise from the ashes of the worst.

At some point most of us come to the conclusion that we have three choices: give up, give in, or give it all you've got. We get to decide which path we will take. Recently I heard a thought-provoking comment, "No matter what life gives you, give more back."

Mike McTigue, a lacrosse teammate and close friend of Chris, offers a friend's perspective. Mike wrote a song as he struggled up the steep mountain of carving out a life without Chris:

I took a drive by myself one day about a year after Chris
disappeared. . .
Sat by the banks of the Root River
Saw the leaves all changing color
Right about then I began to wonder. . .

In a sense, I've gotten older
Innocence, I'm still a youngster
In a sense, life should be cookin'
In a sense...
I'm still lookin'
In the bushes
In the river
It's gettin' clearer...
Gonna have to find him in the mirror.

My own plan is to continue to live my life with as much purpose and joy as I can. To create a more promising future, we must continue to face forward and focus on the road ahead. We must believe Chris is in a better place and will always be with us; trust Chris loves us dearly and wants us to be happy; acknowledge our contribution to Chris's remarkable life; trust we have left meaningful footprints; continue to focus on our current family (Sara, Jamie, Cayman Rose, and Jace Christopher); create a life worth living; express gratitude; believe our family will be together again; and accept Jesus's peace: "Peace I leave with you; My peace I give to you . . . Do not let your hearts be troubled and do not be afraid." —John 14–27 (ESV)

For more information regarding our decade of fighting for justice, read my 2009 book, *Footprints of Courage,* available on amazon.com.

Learn more about Chris's remarkable life at http://legacyofcourage.com/legacy/honoring-chris.

CHAPTER 20

DICK: *GRIEF REVISITED*
by The Reverend Elaine Barber

David writes:

The Reverend Elaine Barber, an Episcopal priest and avid outdoor voyager, called me after our son Jon went missing. We grew over time to be friends and fellow admirers. Elaine is an active supporter of the Jon Francis Foundation. Her presentation at one of our annual fundraising events was moving and memorable. People often refer to her story and her words of wisdom. Her talk superbly captured the purpose of JFF. I have yet to meet anyone who so completely understands the risks, rewards, and heartache that the wilderness can deliver.

"Minnetonka couple's dream canoe trip turns to nightmare," an article by Mary Lynne Smith in the *Star Tribune* on June 7, 2013, described Elaine's last canoe trip with her husband Dick. "Plunged into frigid waters on Sunday, Elaine Barber thought, *I have to make it*. Her husband didn't. Dick Barber, 78, was lost Sunday in the cold Basswood River when he and his wife, Elaine, capsized while on a three-week canoe trip." The articled ended with her words of advice to adventurers, "Be prepared. Take emergency devices. Praise your rescuers."

Elaine writes:

Dick died on the first day of our canoe trip to the Crooked River area of the Quetico Park in Canada more than five years ago. We had spent twenty years on similar canoe trips, so we had no anxiety about the anticipated venture. It was early in the season, June 2, but we wanted to enjoy the entire month of June in the Quetico before returning to Ely for July at our Vermilion College Apartment, our summer home for the last two decades.

Many of our trips in that area of the wilderness, in the more western side of the Quetico, had been later in the summer when the rivers move at a slower pace. We certainly did not imagine that the flow of the water would be as strong as it was on that day. The map I had with us on that day did not show the portage as clearly as one of the maps I must have left behind in the apartment. I knew we needed to be close to the Minnesota side of the river. But we drifted out too far from shore, and before we knew it, we were in trouble!

We moved forward at a rate we had never seen in past years, and that should have been a warning to us. The canoe continued to pull us into the area of danger toward a small waterfall we did not see ahead of us. When we entered the turbulent area, our canoe capsized. As soon as the canoe overturned, I grabbed a pack and swam to the closest shore on Canada's side. I believed that Dick would hold onto the canoe and follow me. But tragically, the canoe sailed away from his grip.

When I made it to safety, I turned and saw that Dick was trapped in the rapid area of the river. The canoe was in a pond area close to where I set the packs that had served as my life preservers. I shouted for him to come closer to shore. His response was, "I cannot move."

I believe hypothermia had seized his body.

When I finally made it to the location where I could make my attempt to rescue him in the canoe, he was gone from my sight. His life preserver was on the surface of the water, but Dick was gone. I was alone and still in danger. I needed to grab as much as I could from our supplies and head back to shore.

When I reached the shoreline, I found the SPOT PLB (personal locator beacon) in the backpack, which was a gift from my sons. I sent out a distress signal to the government authorities for a rescue. But the helicopter the Canadian government sent to rescue me circled around the Minnesota side of the river.

So I spent that night alone in a tent under my sleeping bag in dry clothing. The temperature dropped to 33 degrees that evening. I actually slept well after turning off the SPOT PLB as darkness and evening slipped over that beautiful riverbank.

Why I was so calm and comfortable that evening? I do not know exactly. I kept saying to myself, *Help will come in the morning.*

When I woke the next morning, the fog was starting to clear and the helicopter arrived. Government authorities had contacted one of my sons, and they authorized a search-and-rescue operation. Among the many details from that day, the most important was the presence of an eagle under the helicopter as it took me to safety. That eagle for me was God's presence that day. Working for the last forty years with the native community, I know the importance of the eagle as a symbol and a guide to God's creation and care.

I could site many Bible verses that have guided me through these last five years. One of them is from Proverbs 3: "Trust in the Lord with all your heart and lean not on your own understanding, but acknowledge God, and God will make straight your path."

My work in world religions as a teacher at Breck School in Minneapolis gave me a way forward through my grief these last five years. In my daily meditation book, *365 Tao Reflections*, is a wisdom saying: "Disasters may well change us deeply, but they will pass. We must keep to our deeper convictions and remember our goals. Whether we remain ash or become the phoenix is up to us."

The example given to me as a science teacher is that the destroyed forest can come back with new life and new growth. I witnessed that fact on a study grant to Yellowstone with my students after a fire in the 1980s. That trip gave me hope to address my new life without my precious canoe partner, Dick Barber. The meditation book also used these words to provide hope in the future. The process of healing takes time, and the process of balance in nature is at the heart of all healing. The wise must be patient in illness, calamity, anger, and healing.

One of the most important sayings that I have lived with for these last five years came from my own belief system, which has guided me well in my eighty years of life. Be grateful for what you have in life and not be angry about what you do not have now. Gratitude is the key to happiness each and every day. The book, *Gratitude*, by Henry Van

Dyke states the exact idea. I am so grateful for the thirty-one years that I loved Dick Barber, and I cannot be upset or angry that I was not given more time with him as my husband and companion in life.

We married on June 2, and Dick died on June 2, 2013, our anniversary. We had just eaten lunch together on the Shore of Basswood Lake, where he opened an anniversary card. That was a gift to both of us, and it was a moment in time to celebrate!

Each one of us has grief in our lives due to so many factors that can visit us on a daily basis. Some of the times and places I miss Dick the most, and react to on an emotional level, are when I am seeing, listening, or doing something that I know Dick would also love to experience. Listening to beautiful music, attending a concert with songs he knew and loved, watching his relatives perform on stage using their family musical talent in the entertainment industry, and being in a wilderness setting to experience the places that we both loved and enjoyed bring me to tears of joy and sadness. Again, I can only stay in the grief mode for a short period of time, then my heart and soul allow me to go back to a happier state of mind.

Another healing gift to me was given from several of my sons and one grandson. They have made sure that each year since Dick's death, I have been able to spend some time in the canoe country that Dick and I loved so much. It's not possible to head to the wilderness for an entire month with their work schedules, but they set aside long weekends and even longer times to be my paddling partners in the Quetico or the Boundary Waters Canoe Area. I am so grateful for that gift to me.

Grief and gratitude must be combined in my life. I do realize that life will never be the same without my "best canoe partner," but it is the gratitude for the years we shared together and the memories of those years that allow me to celebrate the life I shared with him. God has been good to me, and so I am thankful and praise God's name in my life. *Alleluia!*

EPILOGUE

Way back in the Introduction, I wrote that my hope and purpose for writing *Grief Travelers* were that it may comfort, help, inspire, and empower my fellow grief travelers; and also that it will support healthcare practitioners, clergy, and counselors in their important mission to listen and to heal.

I hope that you found some comfort and help in *Grief Travelers*. The Grief Resources section is rich with resources to consult while you are traveling through the valley.

I am deeply grateful for the care I have received and continue to experience from my loved ones, family, my circle of friends, and the many directors, past and present, of the Jon Francis Foundation, who still, today, walk with me through the valley of grief. Thank you to my fellow grief travelers who worked patiently with me on this labor of love and contributed their stories in Part III.

My excellent editor, Marly Cornell, who wrote a book about her daughter Cody who lived with and died from spina bifida (*The Able Life of Cody Jane: Still Celebrating*), further reminded me of the importance of gratitude. After thirteen years, since Jon's death, gratitude is finally creeping into my thoughts. In my church, we often refer to having an attitude of gratitude. A sense of gratitude is good for our emotional health. I think it promotes a positive mental attitude. Over time, I have slowly replaced some of my sorrow with gratitude. Many others have talked with me about the same process. We dwell less on what we lost and more often on a feeling of gratitude for what we once had.

Jon was kind and compassionate toward me. He made me feel proud, and he inspired me. Jon brought relentless happiness into my world by how he lived his brief life—he lived joyfully and loved boldly.

I remember a conversation with another father who said, "I will be happy if my children don't grow up and go off to prison." I agreed but thought those were low expectations. Not only did Jon do no harm in his life, but he also served others in a vibrant ministry. He was a strong, healthy, and gifted athlete, so a number of my most vivid recollections are of him running with joy and tenacity. Jon ran and climbed for the sheer enjoyment and for the Glory of God.

As he was a man of faith, I envision Jon sitting at the right hand of God, discussing theology. Perhaps he is taking a writing class from Isaiah and running the "Pearly Gate Marathon" each year.

Jon, thank you for your unconditional love for me and for your gift of countless happy memories. I will be forever grateful to you, and I look forward with joy and anticipation to joining you in life eternal.

At Jon's funeral, Jon's friend Alex read a poem that Linda had shared with Jon from a book called *Stars in Your Bones: Emerging Signposts on Our Spiritual Journeys* by Alla Bozarth, Julia Barkley, and Terri Hawthorne. The poem was one of Jon's favorites and movingly reflected the kind of love Jon gave so freely.

BIODANCE

Everything bears the property of Love—
    Sitting on a rock in the Salmon River
    watching first leaves fall.

From sun-high mountain treetops
upstream the rapids carry
old branches to the sea,
their leaves landlocked already.
Why so soon?
Not soon at all—
your time is complete.
And so is mine.

You rest in sunlight
before transforming
into earth and air.

You dissolve your leafy form
and recompose into a thousand bodies.

Nothing ever ends.
Everything is always
beginning.

Shall I find myself tomorrow

shining in a water drop
on a piece of moss
on the bark of a tree
that once was you?

Green into burnt red,
old leaf, our biodance began
millennia ago, but today
I am glad to see you clearly
for the first time
with just these eyes,
my changing
partner!
Your bronze body
Turns to powder
with a crack
beneath my foot.

Part of you has already become me.
You are on your new way.

You will be back.
And so will I.
    So will I.

—Alla Bozarth

As the great grandson of an Irish immigrant,
I say farewell to you with this Irish blessing:

In time of sorrow . . . May you see God's light on the path ahead
when the road you walk is dark.
May you always hear, even in your hour of sorrow,
the gentle singing of the lark.
When times are hard, may hardness never turn your heart to stone.
May you always remember when the shadows fall—
you do not walk alone. Peace to you!

—David

RESOURCES ON GRIEF AND LOSS

The unexpected, tragic, and sudden death of our twenty-four-year-old son, Jon, inflicted on us the deepest, most agonizing pain and loss we have ever known. To survive, work through, and cope with it, Linda and I sought comfort, healing, and understanding from our faith, authors, "authorities," and others who have walked through the valley of the shadow of grief.

Attig, Thomas. *How We Grieve: Relearning the World.* Oxford: Oxford University Press, Inc. 1996.

Bernstein, Judith R. *When the Bough Breaks: Forever After the Death of a Son or Daughter.* Kansas City, Missouri: Andrews and McMeel. 1997.

Blair, PhD, Pamela D., and Brook Noel. *I Wasn't Ready to Say Goodbye: surviving, coping & healing after the sudden death of a loved one.* Naperville, Illinois: Sourcebooks, Inc. 2008.

Boss, Pauline. *Ambiguous Loss: Learning to Live with Unresolved Grief.* Cambridge, Massachusetts: Harvard University Press. 1999.

Boss, Pauline. *Loss, Trauma and Resilience: Therapeutic Work with Ambiguous Loss.* New York: W.W. Norton & Company. 2006.

Bozarth, Alla Renee. *Life is Goodbye Life is Hello: Grieving Well Through All Kinds of Loss.* Center City, Minnesota: Hazelden Foundation. 1994.

Bozarth, Alla Renee. *A Journey through Grief: Gentle, Specific Help to Get You through the Most Difficult Stages of Grieving.* Center City, Minnesota: Hazelden Foundation. 1990.

Brach, Tara. *Radical Acceptance: Embracing Your Life with the Heart of a Buddha.* New York, New York: Bantam Books. 2003.

Braestrup, Kate. *Here If You Need Me*. New York: Back Bay Books/Little, Brown and Company. 2007.

Bush, Michael D. *This Incomplete One: Words Occasioned by the Death of a Young Person*. A collection of sermons. Grand Rapids, Michigan: William B. Eerdmans Publishing Company. 2006.

Chittister, Joan D. *Scarred by Struggle, Transformed by Hope*. Grand Rapids, Michigan: William. B. Eerdmans Publishing Company. 2005.

Chodron, Pema. *When Things Fall Apart: Heart Advice for Difficult Times*. Boston, Massachusetts: Shambhala Publications, Inc. 1997.

Didion, Joan. *A Year of Magical Thinking*. New York: Vintage Books, a division of Random House, Inc. 2005.

Emmons, Henry. *Chemistry of Joy: A Three-Step Program for Overcoming Depression Through Western Science and Eastern Wisdom*. New York, New York: Fireside. 2006.

Emmons, Henry. *Chemistry of Calm: Settle your Mind, Reclaim Health Emotions, Stop Worrying and Start Fully Living!* New York, New York: Touchstone. 2010.

Farr, Rev. Mary I. *If I Could Mend Your Heart*. Minneapolis, Minnesota: Shorehouse Books. August 2017. [Mary is an Episcopal deacon and a hospital chaplain. Simple and beautiful. Patty and Jerry Wetterling sent us her original version of this book in 2006.]

Fisher, Bruce and Robert Alberti. *When your Relationship Ends*. Anta Clarita, California: Impact Publishers. 2003. [Marketed as a divorce book, but really a grieving book.]

Francis, David. *Bringing Jon Home: The Wilderness Search for Jon Francis*. Edina, Minnesota: Beaver's Pond Press, Inc. 2010. [Memoir about the life, loss, and legacy of an uncommon young man.]

Friedman, Russell and John W. James. *The Grief Recovery Handbook: The Action Program for Moving Beyond Death, Divorce, and Other Losses.* New York: Harper Collins Publishers. 2009.

Hanh, Thich Nhat. *Peace Is Every Step: The Path to Mindfulness in Everyday* Life. New York, New York: Bantam Books. 1991.

Hickman, Martha Whitmore. *I Will Not Leave You Desolate.* Nashville, Tennessee: Abingdon Press. 1982.

Hickman, Martha Whitmore. *Healing After Loss, Daily Meditations for Working through Grief.* New York: HarperCollins Publishers. 1994.

Jenkins, Jan. *Footprints of Courage: Our Family's Struggle for Justice.* Savage, Minnesota. Heaven's Ink, Inc. 2009.

Kubler-Ross, MD, Elisabeth. *On Death and Dying.* New York: Simon and Schuster, Inc. 1969.

Kubler-Ross, MD, Elisabeth. *Questions and Answers On Death and Dying.* New York: Macmillan Publishing Company, Inc. 1974.

Lindemann, MD, Erich. *Beyond Grief: Studies in Crisis Intervention.* New York: Jason Aronson, Inc. 1979.

Mazur, Kim Owen. *Losing My Reflection: A Coloring Book Journal to Record Your Personal Grief Experience.* Edina, Minnesota: Beaver's Pond Press, Inc. 2018.

Nouwen, Henri J. M. *The Dance of Life: Weaving Sorrow and Blessings into one Joyful Step.* London: Darton, Longman and Todd and Notre Dame, Indiana: Ave Maria Press. 2005.

Oates, Joyce Carol. *A Widow's Story: A Memoir.* New York: HarperCollins Publishers. 2011. [A great book full of raw emotions and clearly followed the sequence of events for coping with death in the first year.]

Rando, Therese A. *How To Go On Living When Someone You Love Dies.* New York: Bantam Books. 1991.

Rosof, Barbara D. *The Worst Loss: How Families Heal from the Death Of A Child.* New York: Henry Holt and Company, LLC. 1994.

Rupp, Joyce. *Walk in a Relaxed Manner: Life Lessons from the Camino.* New York: Maryknoll. 2005.

Schwiebert, Pat. *Tear Soup: A Recipe for Healing After Loss.* Grief Watch, 5th Edition, 2005. [affirms the bereaved, educates, and is a building block for children (adults too)]

Seftick, Dan. *Real Mountains: The Story of an Inspired Life*. Edina, Minnesota: Beaver's Pond Press, Inc. 2016. ["The grief from the death of a child is the greatest grief. Nothing can match it. The trick is to move through the grief and not remain stuck. This is a monumental task for an individual to face. The truth is this task does not have to be faced alone." —Dan Seftick.]

Strommen, Merton P. and Irene A. *Five Cries of Grief: One Family's Journey to Healing after the Tragic Death of a Son.* Minneapolis, Minnesota: Augsburg Fortress Publishers. 1996.

Westberg, Granger E. *Good Grief: A Companion for Every Loss.* Minneapolis, Minnesota: Fortress Press. 2019.

Westra, Mary Rondeau. *After the Murder of My Son.* St. Cloud, Minnesota: North Star Press. 2010.

Wolterstorff, Nicholas. *Lament for a Son.* Grand Rapids, Michigan: Wm. B. Eerdmans Publishing Company. 1987.

Worden, J. William. *Grief Counseling and Grief Therapy: A Handbook for the Mental Health Practitioner.* New York: Springer Publishing Company. 1991.

The Bible, (NIV) Old Testament Book of Job. Isaiah 55:9. New Testament, Matthew 25:34–40, Romans 8:18, John 16:33, James 1:12. [And much more].

Websites

Devine, Megan. www.refugeingrief.com [She has just released her latest book, *It's OK That You're Not OK: Meeting Grief & Loss in a Culture that Doesn't Understand.* She also has a web-based support/writing group.]

Emmons, Henry. *Partners in Resilience.* www.partnersinresilience.com/who-we-are/henry-emmons.

The Compassionate Friends. www.thecompassionatefriends.org [Through a network of over 600 chapters with locations in all fifty states, as well as Washington DC, Puerto Rico, and Guam, The Compassionate Friends has provided support to bereaved families after the death of a child for four decades.]

Grief Recovery Institute. www.griefrecoverymethod.com. Russell Friedman and John W. James wrote *The Grief Recovery Handbook* ["There is a high probability that you, or someone you love, is suffering from a broken heart. Is it due to a death, divorce or another major loss? If so you might feel sad, distracted, or confused. You are not alone. The Grief Recovery Method has been helping people feel better following a loss for forty years."]

GriefShare www.GriefShare.org is for people grieving the death of a family member or friend. GriefShare groups meet weekly. Each session includes 1) video seminar with experts, 2) focused support group discussion, and 3) personal study and reflection.

Kabat-Zinn, Jon. Guided Mindfulness Meditation Practices with Jon Kabat-Zinn. https://www.mindfulnesscds.com

Keating, Thomas. *Centering Prayer.*
https://www.contemplativeoutreach.org/fr-thomas-keating

Lessons Learned in Life. www.lessonslearnedinlife.com [Positive quotes "To encourage you to keep going."]

Mayo Clinic Website. https://www.mayoclinic.org/diseases-conditions/complicated-grief/symptoms-causes.

The National Suicide Prevention Lifeline provides free confidential support 24/7 for people in distress, including prevention and crisis resources, and best practices for professionals. 1-800-273-8255 https://suicidepreventionlifeline.org

Open to Hope. www.opentohope.com. Open to Hope ® is a nonprofit with the mission of helping people find hope after loss. "Giving a Voice to Grief and Recovery."

ABOUT THE AUTHOR

David Francis is the award-winning author of *Bringing Jon Home* about the search for his twenty-four-year-old son who went missing in 2006 while climbing the Grand Mogul in the Sawtooth Mountains of Central Idaho. Francis is a retired US Navy captain (nuclear submarine service), businessman, and adjunct business professor.

Francis is executive director of the Jon Francis Foundation, which is dedicated to saving lives through wilderness safety education, empowering families who have suffered the loss of an adult loved one in the wilderness, and advocating for legal protection for missing adults.

www.jonfrancisfoundation.org

Francis is a husband to Linda, father to Jon, Melissa, Jocelyn, and Robin, and grandfather to Camille, Charlie, Audrey, Steven, Katie, and Taylor. David and Linda live and love in Stillwater, Minnesota.

Made in the USA
Lexington, KY
05 December 2019